BATTLES OVER BRITAIN

The Archaeology of the Air War

This book is dedicated to the memory of Sgt Paul Klipsch and all his colleagues in No. 92 (East India) Squadron who lost their lives in the Battle of France, the Battle of Britain and the other aerial conflicts of the Second World War.

BATTLES OVER BRITAIN

The Archaeology of the

Air War

Guy de la Bédoyère

TEMPUS

First published 2000

PUBLISHED IN THE UNITED KINGDOM BY:

Tempus Publishing Ltd
The Mill, Brimscombe Port
Stroud, Gloucestershire GL5 2QG

PUBLISHED IN THE UNITED STATES OF AMERICA BY:

Tempus Publishing Inc.
2A Cumberland Street
Charleston, SC 29401

Tempus books are available in France, Germany and Belgium from the following addresses:

Tempus Publishing Group	Tempus Publishing Group	Tempus Publishing Group
21 Avenue de la République	Gustav-Adolf-Straße 3	Place de L'Alma 4/5
37300 Joué-lès-Tours	99084 Erfurt	1200 Brussels
FRANCE	GERMANY	BELGIUM

British Library Cataloguing in Publication Data.
A catalogue record for this book is available from the British Library.

ISBN 0 7524 1485 2

Typesetting and origination by Tempus Publishing.
PRINTED AND BOUND IN GREAT BRITAIN.

Contents

Illustrations

TEXT FIGURES

COLOUR PLATES

Preface

The Battle of Britain and the Blitz must be two of the most popular subjects for history books; so why another one? This one is written from a completely different tack. As an historian and archaeologist I am fascinated by the proximity of one of the most significant phases in British history which is accessible through written history, contemporary documents, the physical remains of the military hardware and its consequences, and the chance to hear about it from people who were there. What interests me above all else is what the period has to tell us about how all these forms of evidence complement and contradict one another, and what that has to tell us about other periods for which we have nothing like so much material to work from. This should be of interest to historians of any period and also to archaeologists who spend so much of their time necessarily unable to assess what is no longer accessible to them. The book is thus both a history and an archaeology book and I have tried to weave a thread between these diverse forms of evidence.

However, it should be made clear from the outset that archaeology as a discipline has scarcely been applied to the remains of aircraft. Although vast numbers of wrecked aircraft have been dug, and relics removed, virtually none of this has been recorded in any form apart from private photographs. Some excavators have gone to a lot of trouble in recent years to see their efforts documented in book form, and this has rectified part of the problem. Aviation archaeology is consequently in a state which resembles more conventional archaeology as it was more than a century ago in the days of the weekend barrow-digging antiquarian rural vicars. But the wreckage of aircraft is also entirely different, because the history of the time in which they were used is well known and well recorded, which puts the subject into a very interesting context.

The air war in western Europe between 1939 and 1941 has acquired a mythical quality, one which was already to a large extent in existence at the time itself. I have tried in the first instance to understand the aspects and events of the period which helped create this sense of occasion. Beyond that there is the chronology of the period, and the men and materials which characterised it. This was the age of the air-raid shelter, the fighter pilot, and the celebrated Spitfire, an artefact with an image so potent that it came to symbolise all military aircraft during the war. Now, sixty years later, surviving Spitfires command astronomical prices and are routinely displayed to audiences around the world. But the vast majority of Spitfires, and all the other aircraft used in 1939 to 1945 fell out of the sky and were destroyed or scrapped. This takes us to the third part of the story: the archaeological manifestation of the air war at the end of the twentieth century. The questions are: what should we do with it? What does it tell us? And, if this was all we had, what would we make of it? For this aspect of the story I have extended the discussion to include examples and topics from later in the war. The arrival of vast numbers of American aircraft, especially from 1942 onwards, has provided many other instances of air crashes which illustrate more problems of interpretation and excavation or recovery and it would be foolish to ignore them.

In the end it is difficult to avoid the conclusion that the archaeologist is normally so distanced from the world he or she is exploring, and the archaeological evidence so minuscule a remnant, that it is debatable whether archaeology can ever comprehend the past as a human experience without historical evidence to validate or even create interpretations. A little knowledge is a dangerous thing, but a little knowledge is all the archaeologist can normally hope to have. The air war is one part of our past where we can observe all the facets of the evidence, and see how this works.

It has been my privilege to meet and talk to people for whom these early years of the war formed the most extraordinary part of their long lives. I would like to thank in particular Peter Olver and Allan Wright, of Nos. 603 and 92 Squadrons respectively during the Battle of Britain. I would also like to thank Peter Kirk of the Rolls-Royce Heritage Trust whose patient trawls through archives have yielded many interesting pieces of information about the manufacture of this fundamental part of the air war, and the fates of many engines. Gratitude is also due to Simon Parry, Steve Vizard and John Manning, whose various degrees of involvement with the *After the Battle* books on the period and aviation archaeology made it possible for them to answer a number of arcane queries. Simon Stevens drew my attention to the building work at Hawkinge and kindly invited me to visit the archaeological watching brief on the former airfield. Finally, I would like to thank the writer and journalist Elmer Bendiner for his kindness in reading the book and writing an epilogue. Elmer Bendiner was a navigator with the Eighth Air Force's 379th Bombardment Group at Kimbolton (near Huntingdon). Arriving in the UK in 1943 he was well placed to witness Britain's state in the immediate aftermath of the Blitz while at the same time knowing that Britain's survival had made his part in the offensive possible. At once a participant in the air war, and yet able to view the post-Blitz world with a sense of detachment, he has also seen the aircraft of his youth enter the lore of a later age and become a new facet of archaeology.

Like so many people born after the war I have spent much of my life transfixed by the history of events which not only dictated the form of the world in which I grew up, but were also so dramatic that my own life seems unavoidably opaque by comparison. As the twentieth century draws to a close it seems that this fascination is one which is widely shared. For myself it was no less evident while standing in a field in France in the summer of 1999. In a hole before me were the excavated remains of a Spitfire which fell in the Battle of France in May 1940. Above, an intact 57-year-old Spitfire flew rolls in honour of the pilot who died there. And watching with me and dozens of other archaeologists, historians and technicians, was a former RAF pilot who was there that day in 1940, together with men and women of the village who had seen the dogfight and its tragic outcome. Many of the participants had had no expectation of their feelings until that moment.

This book grew directly from that experience and my realisation that the convergence of so many interests and feelings, not least the sheer beauty of the Spitfire itself, would be of interest to a much wider audience. I hope I have succeeded.

Guy de la Bédoyère, Eltham 2000

1 Myth

The creation of legend

At the end of the twentieth century, the 'Blitz' and 'The Battle of Britain' are enduring phrases in common British parlance. Like 'Dunkirk' they have proved a satisfying way of invoking pleasant notions of a time of great strife faced with fortitude, vigour and moral superiority. The 'Dunkirk spirit' is a quality still revered and described as such, while some pictures taken during the Blitz remain classic images of a threat met with resilience and great courage (**1**).

The power of the Second World War to awe and fascinate our own generation is relentless and, as our own day-to-day problems seem ever more trivial, this is hardly surprising. As a consummate historical and social experience its magnitude is overwhelming, even sixty years after the events. That the air war caused 60,000 civilian deaths in Britain alone, and injured some 86,000, remains breathtaking. The effect on Britain's city centres and architecture was unprecedented. Consequently, books on the subject are appearing at an ever greater rate, especially as we approach the inevitable end of living memory. For the same reason television network controllers are perpetually trapped in a dilemma of wishing to move away from the subject, while knowing that documentaries on almost any aspect of the Second World War guarantee major audiences. The conflict's dominance of twentieth-century history only focused more attention on its effect as the millennium drew to a close.

The legends were created in their own lifetime. Churchill's acknowledgement in the summer of 1940 that the Battle of Britain was about to begin, now that France had fallen, enshrined the next few months before they had even happened. The fighter pilots of the period, despite their youth and exhaustion, had no doubt of what the country faced. After the Battle was over and won by the end of October, the Ministry of Information issued in 1941 a pamphlet called *The Battle of Britain*. The account finished with photographs of German bombers lying destroyed on the beach and the words, 'Such was the Battle of Britain in 1940. Future historians may compare it with Marathon, Trafalgar and the Marne.' In late 1940 a biography of Churchill by Hugh Martin appeared called, with a timely eye to the market and the moment, just 'Battle'.

Schoolboys and gung-ho magazines

Considering what was yet to come, the sense of occasion is impressive and no less compelling now than it was at the time. A schoolboy called Colin Perry wrote in his diary:

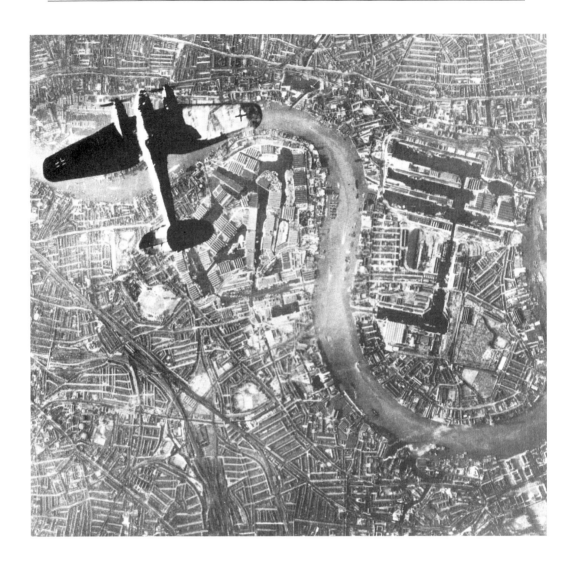

1   *A Luftwaffe Heinkel He 111 twin-engined bomber over south-east London at 1748 on 7 September 1940. This picture is frequently used, but bizarrely hardly ever in the correct orientation. Here north is at the top and the Isle of Dogs is clearly visible to the right (east). On the south bank (lower right) is the Royal Naval College at Greenwich. The two main roads running parallel across the lower left sector are the Old Kent Road and Evelyn Street respectively. The aircraft is about to fly over Shadwell and Wapping on the north bank of the Thames*

29th September 1940: He [Hitler] fails totally to grasp the morale of our people . . . By God, if London, if England, was over-run by Nazis there would still be a band somewhere, undaunted, fighting. We will never surrender. (Perry 1972)

Perry's recollections were committed to an entirely private record until he published it in later life. A compellingly jubilant account of a youth's experience of the early part of the war, it reflects at once the powerful sense of occasion which characterized his day-to-day life and the sustained normality of working lives. 'I obtained two pieces of a German bomb on the office roof this morning', he primly recorded on 9th September 1940.

Although Perry may have been able to see the consequences of the bombing raids and contrails in the sky marking the dog-fights ('I thought they were Nazis drawing their question marks', ibid., 1 September 1940), the pilot heroes were no less mythical to him than they are to us today. Only occasionally did they emerge from the sky above to pass fleetingly before his eyes,

I saw one fighter (I very much fear ours) rush earthwards. With ever increasing speed it fell, silently, to its last resting ground, amongst the green of Surrey. I had no time to dwell upon the fate of that man . . . (Perry 1972, 7-8 September 1940)

'That man' was almost certainly Squadron Leader C.B. Hull of No. 43 Squadron who fell to his death at Purley, Surrey, at 1645 on Saturday, 7 September 1940, in his Hurricane I, serial number V6641. Such details would have been unavailable to the public at the time. The proliferation of published works on the period, exploiting the vast documentary archives have made it possible to easily identify individuals in such cases. But for Perry in 1940 it was a symbolic occasion, as a metaphorical 'unknown pilot' stood for all the losses of the time.

This is an interesting aspect of the period. Opening a commemorative book on the Battle of Britain today involves instant viewing of images and eulogies of the bravery of the 'Few', and the tragic loss of so many young men in the air, and men and women on the ground. There is no doubt that this accurately reflects and rightfully applauds a sacrifice, the significance of which became apparent as the war proceeded and came to an end.

Yet, the published works of the time reflect precisely the same emotions and feelings, apart from minimizing the cruel realities of the deaths. Various gung-ho magazines recorded the weekly events for the benefit of schoolboys aged from 8 to 80, largely indistinguishable from similar magazines which continued to be sold from the end of the war up to the present day. *The War Weekly*, costing a paltry threepence, recounted details of Britain's military might and contrasted it with the pitiful equipment and manpower available to the Axis powers. The edition of 16 August 1940, appearing at the height of the Battle, placed four of the most famous pilot portraits, taken at Hawkinge in July with remarkable prescience, on its back cover with the heading, 'They shot down 17 Nazi planes in half-an-hour.' Unidentified, their anonymity enhanced by the use of the same flying helmet in each photo, these faces have come to symbolize the very essence of what

2   *Pilot Officer Keith Gillman (1920-40) of No. 32 Squadron. Killed in his Hurricane on 25 August 1940, Gillman's widely-publicized portrait came to symbolize the youth and daring associated with the fighter pilot. Gillman was still only 19 when he died. See also* **12**

the Battle of Britain stood for (**2**). A ready market grew up in ephemera, including the extraordinary 'Scientific Height Finder' (**colour plate 1**). This handy booklet featured scale-silhouette images of aircraft on both sides and a curious cardboard device which the would-be spotter could hold to the sky, measure the wingspan and read-off the altitude.

Official images
It is fascinating to see how the images had already been presented in that guise before the Battle had run even half its course. The most familiar of the images, in fact of Pilot Officer Keith Gillman, is especially poignant. He was killed nine days after the magazine appeared at 7.00pm on Sunday, 25 August 1940. He was then flying with No. 32 Squadron from Biggin Hill. He crashed into the sea in Hurricane I, N2433, and to this day remains officially 'missing'. The rest of the magazine was packed with the kind of ludicrously-optimistic copy which seems naïve today. One story pointed out that Berlin Airport be captured with ease (avoiding going into detail as to why it hadn't been), while another announced that the 'Italian Empire is doomed'. Later on, the Home Guard are depicted making skilfully-imaginative use of homing pigeons. To a modern readership, the image is an irremediable prototype for the long-running BBC television comedy series 'Dad's

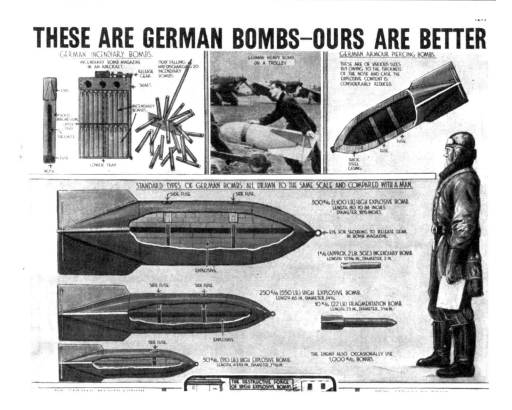

THESE ARE GERMAN BOMBS—OURS ARE BETTER

3   *A page from* War Weekly *of 18 October 1940 providing detailed information about German bombs while pointing out encouragingly their technical defects*

Army'. Two months later, the edition of 18 October ran a feature on German bombing, pronouncing that 'These are German Bombs — Ours are better' (**3**).

To a readership at the time, the reality was the prospect of an armed invasion, and the Home Guard was a fundamental element in the putative defence preparations. The quintessentially tabloid nature of this kind of magazine is predictable and it appealed to a largely practical audience who were, to be fair, presented with a remarkably unsophisticated problem. As one pilot who saw service later in the Battle said to the present author, 'We all thought, well, what a bloody cheek'.

Paul Richey and Richard Hillary
The heroism was, however, also being fostered in an entirely different area. The fact is that many of the RAF pilots, and of course also the Army, and the Navy, were drawn from the upper and middle classes. Many were of exceptional intelligence and highly gifted. If the war had not occurred they would have become politicians, journalists, lawyers, artists, or writers. A number who survived went on to such professions, for example Max Aitken and Hugh Dundas. Some were given the chance to be both during the conflict by imaginative publishers who spied a chance. Necessarily such books came later in the war, but the

4 *F/Lt Paul Richey (1916-89) of No. 1 Squadron, and author of* Fighter Pilot *(1941)*

emergence of *Fighter Pilot* in September 1941, published anonymously (despite illustrating the author and his colleagues) by Batsford had an instantaneous effect. This book was repeatedly reprinted during the war and sales of copies, found today in secondhand bookshops, are often fixed to the time by dated signatures of ownership.

Paul Richey (**4**), as the author was later revealed to be, had produced a dignified, straightforward text which combined the prosaic realities of bleak French fighter airfields for No. 1 Squadron in the British Expeditionary Force, with descriptions of an almost Homeric purity of the induction to aerial combat in the lead-up to the German Blitzkrieg which commenced in May 1940. He recorded a patrol over the border into Germany on 3 March 1940, luxuriating in the peaceful landscape in sight of the Alps, at the controls of his Hurricane I, 'G', N2382:

> This made a very lovely picture, filling me with that curious sensation of aloofness and remoteness that only the pilot knows. It often requires a strong physical effort to wrench oneself away from this dreaming at high altitude, and the mind tends to wander in a curious way . . . Now and again I fired my guns,

5   *F/Lt Richard Hillary (1919-43) of No. 603 Squadron, and author of* The Last Enemy *(1942)*

and was comforted to feel the shudder of the aircraft and to see the converging streams of incendiaries leaping out ahead. (Richey 1941, 18)

Richey's mounting determination to do his duty is no better described than the episode in which an old man, his sons and their team of horses were killed by Germans' bombs. A photo of one of the boys and the team, taken by Richey on a previous occasion, accompanies the text with its caption, 'Military objective at Berry-au-Bac'.

But by the time *Fighter Pilot* appeared in 1941, the Battle of France had already receded from immediate consciousness. The events of the Battle of Britain, had a more compelling last-stand quality. Richard Hillary (**5**) flew with No. 603 (City of Edinburgh) Squadron and participated in the Battle for less than a week before suffering appalling burns in a dog-fight on 3 September 1940. During his long recuperation, which was followed by his death at the controls of a Blenheim on 9 January 1943, he wrote his single book *The Last Enemy*. This appeared in June 1942 and was reprinted constantly throughout the war. It remains in print today. A wartime review in *The Tatler* by Elizabeth Bowen declared it a 'remarkable piece of literature'.

Hillary's book opens with a frantic description of his last sortie during the Battle:

> I felt a terrific explosion which knocked the control stick from my hand, and the whole machine quivered like a stricken animal. In a second, the cockpit was a mass of flames: instinctively, I reached up to open the hood. It would not move. I tore off my straps and managed to force it back; but this took time, and when I dropped back into the seat and reached for the stick in an effort to turn the plane on its back, the heat was so intense that I could feel myself going. (Hillary 1942, 3)

He baled out into the sea after the struggle and floated there for hours waiting for death, the Last Enemy. This forthright confrontation with the ultimate reality of air combat, coupled with his own untimely demise so soon after, catapulted Hillary into literary and wartime immortality. Like Guy Gibson, whose own later career in Bomber Command was preserved in his *Enemy Coast Ahead*, Hillary is forever a young man and pilot, living in a kind of perpetual parallel existence. In his unending Crispin's day our own experiences seem opaque by comparison, and our worries unspeakably trivial.

The Spitfire

Hillary communicated everything that was perceived as glorious about the Battle: the camaraderie, the justness of the cause, and the simple physical beauty of the Spitfire. His tale of the pre-war rowing race, in which the highly-trained and smug Germans were defeated by Hillary's ill-prepared team after one of the Germans spat at them, is a timeless symbol of the carefree competence that he and his like would take to the air. He has been criticized for creating a myth of the playboy fighter pilot, but his image of the Spitfire and its 'wicked beauty' was just one part of the recognition of its potency. As a result of works like these the Spitfire was awarded mythical qualities soon after the machine entered the public arena, and its image became almost a religious icon. This effortless transference from the prosaic war machine into an eternal symbol of valour and human triumph over nature has now granted it a kind of eternal life. The numbers of operational Spitfires are presently at their highest since the early 1950s and are increasing all the time. More than 50 are capable of flying now and frequently command a price in excess of half-a-million dollars on the rare occasions that they change hands. This is a far cry from the £5000-odd the nation paid for each one more than half a century ago. Most of these machines have genuine combat histories, yet have now spent the vast majority of their lives as monuments before being revived to entertain an age which now enjoys the thrills and horrors of war by proxy.

As an artefact the Vickers-Supermarine Spitfire represents an exceptional combination of qualities and peculiarities (**6**). Its physical beauty seems to have been an incidental consequence of the design, though it is unimaginable that this was lost on the man, Reginald Mitchell, who created it, and those who saw it into production. On another level the Spitfire embodied the pinnacle of manufacturing skills and materials available at the time, making it an immensely valuable yardstick by which to measure its age. This becomes particularly apparent when considering the astronomical costs now involved in

6   *Spitfire Mark Is of No. 610 Squadron on patrol in the early spring or summer of 1940. They saw action over Dunkirk during the fall of France. DW-O is serial L1043, transferred to No. 266 Squadron by 18 June 1940 which dates the picture. DW-K is X4067, transferred to No. 222 Squadron on 23 September. It had been badly damaged on 24 August but repairs restored it to service, surviving conversions and remaining in use until a collision in early 1942*

returning any Second World War aircraft to flying condition. At the same time, the willingness with which this is done for Spitfires only acts as a further measure of the machine's quite unparalleled status. It is no exaggeration to say that it is the most famous aeroplane ever designed and built, and it may well be true that it is the most famous machine ever built. Of the many eulogies, Brian Kingcome's is both succinct and to the point. His career and survival in Nos. 92 and 72 Squadrons had depended on the machine. Towards the end of his life he recalled that the 'Spitfire personified symmetry and grace. She was a thing apart, defying comparison' (Kingcome 1999, 63).

In this respect the Spitfire is both symbolic and synonymous with the Battle of Britain and the nation's struggle for survival during the Blitz, even though it played a much lesser role against the night bombing. Throughout this book the machine appears again and again because of these factors. There is no intention to belittle the efforts made by the pilots and manufacturers of Hawker Hurricanes and lesser-known machines such as the Boulton-Paul Defiant. The Hurricane bore the brunt of the Battle of Britain in proportion to its greater numbers, and ease and cheapness of its manufacture, maintenance and repair. But even at the time the Hurricane was marginalized from the myth in popular imagery. This may seem difficult to understand, either to someone who did not live at the time or who is not familiar with the aircraft of the Second World War. It becomes palpably self-evident to anyone watching a flying Spitfire in our own time. Its form is so unparalleled, not just at the time but before and since, that its qualities cannot be unappreciated. In the war there were 'Spitfire Funds' but not 'Hurricane Funds'. Today only a very few Hurricanes still fly.

History and archaeology

Not surprisingly the books by Richard Hillary and Paul Richey are only two of many on similar themes produced during the war and afterwards, though as works of literature they remain often imitated but never equalled. All constitute sources for the period although dimmed memories and time introduce inconsistencies. Even Hillary's text is not easy to reconcile precisely with official records of losses. But this is not really the long-term value of these books. They represent eye-witness accounts of a type and quality rarely available for any period.

Hillary of course is no longer with us. Richey survived the war but died in 1989. Richey's colleague in No. 1 Squadron, John 'Killy' Kilmartin, who also trained Hillary in Spitfires, died in October 1998. Their passing represents the coming to an end of first-hand recollections of the greatest human experience of the twentieth century. This makes books like Alfred Price's *The Hardest Day* (1979) all the more valuable. Benefiting from original documents and photographs, post-war revelations, living memory from both sides and hindsight, its coverage of a single day, 18 August, in the Battle of Britain is in many ways a more useful account of the period July to October 1940 than the plethora of books which profess to provide the 'definitive' record.

Aviation archaeology
Nevertheless, the sheer volume of recorded history of the Second World War has almost completely marginalized its archaeology. It is truly astonishing to see how little of that archaeology actually survives. Here we have the chance to compare the history and the documentation with what remains extant. As an example, of the tens of thousands of aircraft manufactured, only a few score remain. A single Spitfire which saw action in the Battle of Britain still takes to the air and even that is scarcely the same physical machine. No Hurricane of the Battle of Britain still flies. Apart from a handful which survive as static museum exhibits, the rest lie scattered in the ground or survive as excavated scrap in private museums (**7**). The rest were long since melted down.

In fact, it is has been almost exclusively the work of the much-reviled aviation archaeologist that has preserved any of this at all. From the 1960s onwards bands of diggers, variously described as 'aviation enthusiasts', 'relic-hunters', and 'grave-robbers', embarked on searching out the fallen aircraft and digging them up. Making use of an imaginative combination of official documents, local information and field-walking, they proceeded to track down vast numbers of crashed aircraft of the Battle of Britain and other aspects of the air war.

In general the remains found their way to private museums, some of which remain open to the public. A host of issues rose to the fore, including ownership of the physical remains of the aircraft and, more importantly, whether or not remains of the pilot were

7   *Rocker-cover fragment from the Rolls-Royce Merlin engine fitted to Hurricane I, V6782, of No. 229 Squadron which was shot down over Burwash (East Sussex) on 27 September 1940. F/Lt R. Rimmer was killed. This was one of the few pieces of evidence found on the crash site. Now at Sandown*

left in the wreckage. In general the exhumation of human remains (not in fact very common) was welcomed by families and treated with considerable respect by the excavators. Officialdom and public opinion (at least that of people not related to the deceased airman) often felt differently. There were also colossal problems concerning identification, recording and storage. It is undoubtedly the case that a great deal has been mislaid, misidentified, scrapped or its provenance lost along the way.

To a large extent these issues have become academic. Most of the accessible machines have now been dug anyway. What matters is that the preservation of much of this period, and that includes sections of the airfields, is attributable to, and only to, these groups. One might draw easy comparisons with the nineteenth-century antiquarians whose digs and collections now constitute substantial proportions of the collections of the British Museum and other provincial museums in this country.

The nature of the record

In 1948 a film called *The Guinea Pig* was released. It featured a young Richard Attenborough as a 'common' boy sent to a public school as an experiment. The film is now an intriguing social comment on growing awareness of the problems created by class differences, and the empathy that resulted from the experience of war which threw together people of all backgrounds. One scene features a school service in the chapel and the camera poignantly tracks across to home in on the memorial to the boys of the fictional school who had fallen in the Battle of Britain. Despite this vivid evocation of the potency of the image the memorial states that the Battle had lasted from July 1940 to October 1941.

This of course is at variance with the official end of the Battle on 31 October 1940. Unlike most battles, the Battle of Britain had no straightforward beginning at dawn followed by a day of conflict and a cessation in the twilight of evening. The Battle of Britain was made up of thousands of different battles, fought in seconds rather than minutes high above southern England and over the Channel. Few of those fighting at the end had been involved at the beginning, and along the way hundreds of young men had combat careers which might have lasted moments or months. In the 1941 HMSO booklet the Battle's 'Great Days' were attributed to 8 August to 31 October 1940 by when it had 'died gradually away'. It was not until 1960 that the dates of the Battle were officially fixed at 11 July to 31 October 1940.

The closing date provided by the film then appears to be in error, which seems remarkable considering that anyone working on the film must have lived through the period in question. It demonstrates, or at least symbolizes, how recent events are not so recent that they do not merit examination, investigation and understanding at an historical and archaeological level. By being created as myths in their own time, the Battle of Britain and the Blitz became detached from cast-iron reality.

The problem is compounded by lacunae in the records caused by destruction, loss, or straightforward omissions. Even today, anyone researching the subject in detail swiftly notices streams of inconsistencies in parallel descriptions of the same events appearing in different books. There are dozens of different reasons for this. Memory plays tricks, and printers make errors. And it is also true that the authors of some books on the details of the air war are not by profession historians. One recent reference work on fighter pilots had to be swiftly followed by a further volume containing addenda and corrections so numerous that the original book is useless without it. Elsewhere, pilots' names are subjected to various spellings. The name of Allan Wright, who served with No. 92 Squadron before, during, and after the Battle of Britain, is almost invariably misspelled as Alan, and in one remarkable instance, repeated references to him in a single book as Alan Wright are then followed by a caption describing him as Robert Wright, another individual completely.

A further example involving Wright is the series of photographs of a Spitfire, R6923, of No. 92 Squadron, bearing the squadron code QJ-S (**8**). The Spitfire was a Mark I, converted to Mark V configuration, which is the state it was in when it was photographed in the air. This series of photographs was so extensively used during the war, and after that it must be the single best-recorded individual fighter aircraft of the period. Yet, the majority of captions accompanying various frames from the shoot do not name the pilot. Some state that it was the Squadron Leader of 92 Squadron in the summer of 1941, Jamie Rankin. Only one noted by the present author states that it was flown by Allan Wright and that the session occurred on 19 May 1941 (Freeman 1998, 42-3). The latter is recorded in Wright's log-book, and was an incident he recalled in 1999 to the author. The same squadron's exploits on 23 May 1940, during the fall of France, are featured in one widely-printed and reprinted popular book as occurring on 25 May 1940. A casual glance at the squadron's operation record for the day, stored at the Air Historical Branch, confirms that it took place on the 23rd.

8 *Spitfire V (in this case a modified Mark I), R6923, of No. 92 Squadron, flown by Allan Wright in May 1941, photographed from a Blenheim for a series of publicity photographs*

Considering how recent the Second World War is, it comes as something of a surprise to learn how varied the extant record is. During the war itself a great deal of effort was expended on recording the movement of personnel, hardware and munitions. Individual pilots recorded their daily exploits in their own logbooks which were examined monthly by the squadron leader. The logbooks normally subsist with the surviving pilots or their descendants, though a number have found their way into museums or private collections. The logbook compiled by Robert Stanford Tuck, who flew Spitfires and Hurricanes in the Battle, has been published in facsimile form. Pilots also filled in a Combat Report form which provide personal versions of an air battle in which the squadron was involved. From these a daily report for the squadron was written up in the Operations Record Book (RAF Form 50). These official records survive today in the Public Record Office and the Air

Historical Branch. Collectively, they generally make it possible to reconstruct the basic sequence of events on any given day. Occasionally it is possible to collate RAF records with equivalent Luftwaffe accounts.

As far as aircraft were concerned the machines were recorded in the factories where they were made, and also by the RAF when they took them 'on charge'. Some of the components, principally the engine, were also recorded by the manufacturers. Most of these aircraft came to grief before the end of the war, and their individual ends were recorded also, sometimes on fatal accident reports. While this seems promising, the reality is often very different. Early in the war an RAF aircraft's record card (Air Ministry Form 78, **43**) normally carried the serial number or numbers of the engine. This practice rapidly lapsed and the number was omitted. This was quite understandable, given the fact that aircraft which escaped an early demise survived much longer than their engines. But it does mean that an excavated aircraft, which may carry its original engine, cannot be identified from the engine's serial number.

Rituals in the air

Minor though these examples are, they illustrate a problem with detail which might not be expected with events so recent and which subsist (just) in living memory. An example from slightly later in the war describes something which, had it been the speculation of an archaeologist attempting to explain a find, would be regarded as ludicrous and comical. Don Charlwood, sometime navigator on a Lancaster bomber of No. 103 Squadron, flying out of Elsham, recalled the occasion when his crew were obliged to use another machine. The normal 'owners' of T Tommy (the Lancaster's call-sign) were anxious to demonstrate the ritual observances required to ward off disaster. Firstly, it was necessary to rub the belly of a 'gremlin' painted on the fuselage and known as Yohodi. This would, it was promised, guarantee against the guns freezing up. The rubbing of a horseshoe hung over the navigator's table would guard against becoming lost (Charlwood 1984, 144-5).

Charlwood's crew observed the rituals and returned home safely much to the relief of T Tommy's crew whose principal anxiety was the recovery of their beloved mount. The incident reflects not just the youth of the men involved but also a level of anxiety and a feeling of the virtual inevitability of death which our own age cannot possibly contemplate. All Britain's recent conflicts (the Gulf War, and the Balkan Crisis) have involved low casualty rates and no danger whatsoever to the public at home. In contrast, the young men of Bomber Command had, on a statistical basis, virtually no chance at all of surviving their tours of duty (a loss rate of 4 percent meant a statistical likelihood that they would be lost on 1 in 25 missions, the initial length of a tour). Fighter Command's experiences in the early part of the war were not quite so bad but the appearance of new faces on a squadron who had arrived, flown and died before either unpacking their cases or being introduced to their comrades was sadly routine. This intensity of experience undoubtedly helped concentrate the minds of those who lived, each of whom devised his own way of coping. For some, riotous partying and indulgence were the only ways to escape. Tony Bartley's autobiography of his time with No. 92 Squadron, *Smoke Trails in the Sky* (1984), is a conspicuous example of just that.

For others, religion did just as well and somewhere along the way a kind of spiritual

9 *Half-crown coin recovered from the wreckage of a Messerschmitt Bf110C-1 (Wk no. 2837) which crashed at Church Farm, Washington, near Pulborough (West Sussex) on 4 September 1940 (*After the Battle*)*

superstition of a type invoked by the Roman military altars of Hadrian's Wall developed. Charlwood and his crew might have mocked Yohodi and his powers. For their own part, they placed their trust in a 'grimy toy rabbit, which we called "Nunc Nunc"' (op. cit. 146). The fascinating thing about this anecdote is that it validates the theory behind some of the wilder archaeological speculations about 'ritual', even if it does not (and cannot) confirm it in any one instance. The recovery of a British half-crown from the wreckage of a German aircraft takes on a slightly different hue in this context. Was it merely a souvenir, or had it become a crew member's personal talisman (**9**)?

Archaeology and the human experience
At another level this problem of interpretation amply illustrates the paradox of conventional archaeology. By its very nature, the recovery of artefacts cannot possibly recreate the spiritual background or the specific circumstances behind deposition. Necessarily then, the archaeologist is normally condemned to recreating a general background to explain his or her site. Divorced from the immediacy of human experience and the converging circumstances of an occasion, which includes the specific personalities involved, the archaeologist is handicapped from the start. These days, the recognition that circumstances of a sort must have been involved, rather than just a set of background generalities, has allowed speculation about the effect of 'agencies'. This anodyne substitute at one stroke recognizes that the world and its events are dictated by natural phenomena including animals, and people with all their various idiosyncrasies, and also recognizes that

we normally cannot know what those were. The role of a battered toy rabbit in sustaining the equanimity of seven young men could never possibly be recreated by an archaeologist sifting through the wreckage of that bomber (though Charlwood and his crew in fact survived the tour of duty). But at least the fact that their habit was recorded can and must help the more detached recreation of the Roman and prehistoric world.

Of course, the vast majority of finds from wartime air-crash sites, and other pieces of evidence, are far more prosaic. Air crashes consist very largely of piles of scrap metal. Built for speed and lightness, the fighter of the 1940s was superbly strong in one direction (that is, for going forwards), and exceptionally weak for going in any other direction. The trauma of impact normally destroyed the form of the airframe, and the incidence of fire could very easily reduce much of the light alloy metal to powder. Where possible, the wreckage was removed. A police report of 29 September 1940 states that the remains of Hurricane I, P3782, which crashed on 3 September, were 'removed by an RAF Squad with a long, low, loader on Saturday the 26th September'. The evidence for this crash thus subsisted only in the contemporary documentation, apart from the maintenance of a small memorial garden by a local couple until the 1950s. Only investigations in the 1970s succeeded in tying the crash site to the police report and thus the death of P/O R.H. Shaw of No. 1 Squadron that day. It was not even always evident to the recovery teams at the time which machine they were recovering, and this has added to the confusion.

The 'small finds' of an air crash include the personal effects of the pilot such as small change, maps and sometimes even a daily newspaper. Occasionally the documentation will help confirm the identity of a pilot though this is not automatically the case. Sgt Alexander McKay of No. 73 Squadron died in the crash of his Hurricane I, P3224, at White House Farm, North Fambridge, Essex on 5 September 1940. The excavation of his aircraft yielded a map bearing his name and thus provided a reasonably certain piece of evidence. But is it? No. 73 Squadron had six aircraft shot down that day: three were repairable, three were destroyed. Of the latter, two have been excavated. Only one, McNay's, has provided evidence for its identity. The other (P3110, flown by P/O R.D. Rutter who survived) has not, or at least it has not been recorded as having done so.

The impact of chaos

Like all wars, the air war was chaos first and order a poor second. In a real air battle events took place so fast that a quiet sky could in an instant become a terrifying cataclysm of noise, chaos and vertigo and just as quickly revert to silence as aircraft disappeared in opposite directions at relative speeds approaching 600mph. For an inexperienced man, the proportion of whom increased steadily, such episodes all too often resulted in death or serious injury without warning. Ground controllers often had the distressing experience of hearing young men screaming in agony on radio receivers. The survivors honed their tactics and their skills but even for them a chance bullet could spell oblivion. Allan Wright, then serving with No. 92 Squadron, preserved his Spitfire's reflector gunsight, shattered by a German bullet which entered his canopy to the side of his head on 9 September (**colour plates 2, 3**). It bounced obliquely back from his forward bulletproof windscreen and destroyed the gunsight. It could so easily have been a tragedy and for many others it was.

Every little battle was a breathtakingly fast miasma of uncertainties after which no-one

10 A Junkers Ju 87 (Stuka) two-man dive-bomber of I/StG77 plummets groundwards on 18 August 1940. It crashed an instant later at West Broyle, nr Chichester (West Sussex). Both crew were killed

really knew what had happened. The image of a Junkers Ju 87 (Stuka) was captured as it plummeted groundwards; moments before it had been attacking Thorney Island on 18 August 1940 (**10**). The often dry entries in the Operations Record book belie the frantic events that had taken place tens of thousands of feet above the ground. No. 266 'Rhodesia' Squadron recorded the results of an 'engagement' with enemy aircraft on 16 August 1940, including the information that:

> At 1215 hours aircraft ordered from Manston to intercept enemy aircraft. An engagement followed which resulted in the following casualties to personnel and aircraft. Squadron Leader R.L. Wilkinson (No. 26192) piloting Spitfire R6768 found Dead at Eastry nr. Deal, death due to multiple injuries and burns. Sub-Lieutenant H.L. Greenshields (RNVR) piloting Spitfire N3240 missing. Pilot Officer N.G. Bowen (No. 41984) piloting Spitfire N3095 found dead at Adisham nr. Canterbury, death due to multiple injuries and burns. Spitfire P9312 piloted by Flying Officer (Acting Flight Lieutenant) S.N. Bazley, pilot

escaping by parachute landed in a cornfield near Canterbury and was taken to hospital suffering from burns and minor injuries. Spitfire K9864 piloted by Pilot Officer J.F. Soden (No. 42903) hit by shellfire in fuselage and force landed north of Faversham, pilot received slight shrapnel wounds in the leg. Spitfire X4066 delivered by Ferry Pool from No. 8 Maintenance Unit.
(266 Squadron Operations Record Book, RAF Form 540, p. 71)

The 'engagement' had, by any normal account, been a disaster for No. 266 Squadron. Four pilots were killed and one injured in a dogfight with Stab II/JG26 which cost the latter their leader, Hptmn Ebbighausen, in the first few seconds. Moments later the tables were turned. Four Spitfires were destroyed and a fifth, K9864, was eventually repaired though neither she nor her pilot on 16 August survived the war. A sixth, X4030, is unmentioned in the Operational Record but was also damaged though it reached home. The new Spitfire, X4066, was destroyed on the ground at Manston on 18 August, along with another, by strafing Messerschmitt Bf 109s. It had just five flying-hours to its name. Not surprisingly, the squadron was withdrawn from the frontline to Wittering where it remained for the rest of the Battle. Of the machines, Ebbighausen's Bf 109 was lost in the sea, one of the Spitfires crashed in France and the others were either scrapped or repaired. Only Wilkinson's machine has yielded any physical evidence of its crash-site in modern times.

One of the main consequences of the aerial chaos was later recognized to be an over-estimate by both sides of what they had achieved that day. Naturally this was helped along by governments anxious to encourage a belief that the enemy was fighting a hopeless cause. A pilot was inclined to believe that an aircraft at which he had fired, and which then crashed, had been downed by him. It was easy to forget that his colleagues may have participated, or been responsible themselves. This was not always ignored and, as a result, $\frac{1}{2}$ or even $\frac{1}{4}$ shares might be awarded. But it worked both ways. A pilot might have known that he had shot an aircraft down but in the absence of a crash site or other confirmation from the ground he might have to forgo the score.

In practice, for the historian this means it is practically impossible to reconstruct exactly the procession of events in an individual dogfight, or on a single day. Alfred Price's *The Hardest Day*, an account of the events of 18 August 1940, is a conscientious effort to do just that. But the very reliance on recollections by men before 1979, some of whom are no longer with us, only emphasizes the importance of listening while at the same time retaining a healthy regard for the vagaries of memory and the necessity of matching anecdotes with what remains of the various records of the period.

The extent of the evidence
The physical evidence for the air war and the Blitz extends way beyond the remnants of aircraft and their crews. Fighter Command's 11 Group, which covered the south-east, was divided into sectors, each of which contained several airfields (**61**). One of these airfields served as a Sector Station. Thus Biggin Hill, still a household name, was Sector Station for Sector C, an area which extended from roughly where the south-east part of the M25 motorway runs today, right out to the coast from close to Folkestone, and as far west as

Pevensey between Hastings and Eastbourne. Each one of these airfields had fairly similar facilities, though their origins varied.

Almost all had once been farmland which was requisitioned or bought, but some had been originally used as civilian aerodromes. The principal feature was the landing and take-off area. Not all had concrete runways, grass being usually adequate. Kenley, for example, was equipped with concrete runways and taxiways in the summer of 1939. Around the runways, blast pens accommodated aircraft dispersed around the field while the ancillary structures were clustered around the south. Here were the hangars, stores, a petrol dump, an operations room, an officer's mess, married quarters, and accommodation for NCOs and ground staff. At most of the surviving airfields at least some of these buildings survive in some form today, though extremely few are preserved in a way which approximates to their appearance in 1940-1. Duxford, in 12 Group but on the border with 11 Group, was home to (amongst others) No. 19 Squadron, the first equipped with Spitfires. Today it acts as the Imperial War Museum's principal repository of Second World War aircraft and is a major site for airshows. But it narrowly escaped strangulation by the building of the M11 motorway, and the essential installation of museum buildings has surrounded the wartime hangars with new facilities.

Part of the motion picture *The Battle of Britain* (1968) was filmed at Duxford, re-enacting (without actually saying so) the German raid on Kenley on 18 August 1940. Paradoxically, this outstanding effort to preserve the image and events of the Battle involved destroying some of the original evidence. Many of today's flying Spitfires owe their state to the investment made in restoring them to flying condition for the film (including the only flying Spitfire which saw service in the Battle), but one of Duxford's wartime hangars was blown up to create a spectacular climax to the German raid. Other hangars at different locations now serve as light industrial accommodation or as farm buildings. Similarly, the Nissen hut, that ubiquitous swiftly-erected building which served a thousand purposes, is today a structure which generations of pigs have cause to be grateful for.

The graves of the men and women involved in the conflict are scattered far and wide, but their gravestones are poignant reminders of the shortness of their lives. In this respect they have become part of the greater record of human sacrifice throughout the ages. At the Roman fort of Ambleside a tombstone was found in 1962 which recorded the death of Flavius Romanus, aged 35, who was 'killed in the fort by the enemy.' Close to the disappearing remains of the airfield at Hawkinge, in the frontline in 1940, is a small plot in the civic cemetery containing some of the graves of men of both sides who fell, though their stones tell us little about their fates. Only searches through the vast amount of documentation amassed to record the period provides an answer (**colour plates 4, 21**).

Genuine wartime destruction constitutes another part of the evidence. Perhaps it is only appropriate that the Wren church of St Clement Danes in the Strand, now the RAF church, bears such conspicuous evidence of its wartime experience (**88**). The large pitting in the external surface testifies to the explosion of bombs nearby. But similar traces subsist almost all over south-east England and across the cities of the Midlands, the west, and the north-west. Effectively negative evidence, the most obvious signs include uncharacteristic facades in a row of Victorian or Edwardian terraced or semi-detached houses. These occasionally emulate the undamaged houses on either side but it is rare for them to be identical. Where the destroyed house was more recent the match is sometimes better and all but undetectable. An extreme case of the latter is the Langham Hotel in Great Portland Street. During the war a section was destroyed by enemy action and it remained, clumsily patched-up into the 1980s. The building was then in use by the BBC, whose main headquarters at Broadcasting House lies across the road. The Langham was disposed of as part of the BBC's re-invention of itself in the 1990s and the building resumed its role as a prestigious hotel. The extensive renovation work included replacing the damaged section in identical style and form to the lost masonry. Today the work can barely be seen. In contrast, the modern buildings immediately to the east bear witness to a bombsite that gutted a whole block. No attempt was made to emulate the Georgian architecture of Upper Regent Street and the replacements are obvious interlopers.

Apart from these more conspicuous traces of the air war and the bombing, there are countless thousands of artefacts and ephemera which once played their own part and which now gather dust in cellars, attics, or are paraded for sale in antique shops and jumble sales. The ubiquitous air-raid warden's helmet is perhaps the most frequently found, but parts of uniforms, equipment, photographs, magazines and newspapers all go to make up an enormously complex picture **(colour plates 1, 26)**. The Second World War was a conflict fought between continents and nations but it had manifestations at every level of society in the countries affected and even those which were not. Some of this evidence makes a great deal of difference to our understanding and some of it does not. The important point to recognize is that it was played out in and around our own world. Anyone can experiment with collating all the forms of evidence to recreate an impression of what happened, and how and why it occurred. Part of the story is how the detritus of war affected and characterized the experience of life in postwar Britain. Another part of the story is understanding how evidence survives and exists. Our ability to test it with our wealth of documentary evidence provides the archaeologist and historian with the means to compare their skills and seek to understand all of human history of which this exceptional era was only a part.

Falsifying the myth

It is commonplace in archaeology to uncover the work of forgers, or simply cosmetic dressing for effect, which ends up being misleading. The Battle of Britain is a powerful and evocative image, one which a dealer is only too happy to attribute his wares to and one which a collector is only too happy to believe his new acquisition belongs to. The problem has affected all sorts of artefacts, for example Roman coins depicting the victories in Britain, or the series issued by Vespasian and Titus which record the fall of Jerusalem in 70 with the legend *Iudaea Capta*. A section of engine offered for sale in an antiques showroom was described as being 'from a Battle of Britain Hurricane'. Although undoubtedly from a Merlin engine, it lacked the distinctive part number of a Rolls-Royce product and instead carried a part number with the letter P. This marked it as a Merlin engine manufactured under license by the Packard company in the USA. Its origin is thus far more likely to have been later in the war, from a crash involving a North American P-51 Mustang, or one of the other machines which used Packard Merlins,

11 *Control handle with firing button from Hurricane I, P3063, of No. 46 Squadron, based at Stapleford (Essex). Crashed at Canewdon (Essex) on 3 September 1940. P/O H. Morgan-Gray baled out wounded*

including the British Avro Lancaster heavy bomber.

Another example concerns the Spitfire's control handle and firing button. The latter was made of brass, the former magnesium. Magnesium has one exceptional quality which, in the 1940s, made it highly desirable for aircraft components: its lightness. Unfortunately, it is also highly inflammable and decomposes on exposure to the atmosphere. During the war Barbara Griffiths, née Sparks, worked on quality control in a small engineering firm, Huntley and Sparks, in south Wimbledon where magnesium fittings for a variety of military aircraft were manufactured. Not only were fine tolerances difficult to achieve with magnesium-alloy components, but in her experience, and that of other people in similar work, the parts themselves were liable to burst into flames while being made. Hurricane control handles were not made of magnesium (**11**) but Hurricanes are a good deal less 'popular' than Spitfires, reflected in the increasing numbers of operational Spitfires and the scarcity of Hurricanes in the same state. As perhaps the most evocative component of a Spitfire, the control handle is considered to be exceptionally desirable (**plate 5**). Legitimate reproductions are now manufactured because originals are so scarce. It is thus a mystery why the control column and handle of a No. 603 Squadron Spitfire, R6753, have come to be displayed in exceptional condition at Hawkinge. In fact, doubt as to its authenticity circulates but history of the artefact and its provenance are, as is very common, shrouded in obscurity. The fact alone that major pieces of engine found on a second dig of the site showed that the power plant had erupted, makes it exceedingly unlikely that the control column could have survived in almost mint condition. Quite apart from the properties of magnesium, the column was following an exploding engine moving at several hundred miles an hour.

Such obscurity is pivotal to understanding one of the weak parts of the enthusiast base for this field. A large number of excavations were conducted with what can only be regarded with hindsight as slightly undue haste. Part of the reason was the cost and difficulty of operating heavy plant needed to dig large, stable holes. But it is also true that intense, almost paranoiac, rivalry encouraged certain groups to dig as many sites as possible. Incredibly, this sometimes involved several in a single weekend. If it seems impossible that an aircraft could be comprehensively recovered in so short a time, that is precisely because it is impossible. Digs were generally focused on recovering prime items like engines, cockpit equipment, and personal effects. Much was left where it was, and re-digs of some sites in recent years have yielded large components from aircraft thought to have been dug out. There is more than a passing similarity to the nineteenth-century antiquarians who bored their way into ancient burial mounds in search of grave goods. Not unnaturally, careful recording was overlooked in such hasty excavations (barrows and aircraft alike) with reliance being placed on memory. Together with the confusion inherent in the records concerning identity of crashes in close proximity, the result is often a disputed, or lost, provenance. Thus a control handle from Bell Corner, Old Romney, is variously attributed to Hurricanes P3903 and the meaningless N7885.

There is thus a combination of dishonesty and well-meaning confusion and ignorance. Combined with poor recording the result is a not inconsiderable body of material whose provenance is already lost, or will be lost when its owners die or otherwise dispose of it. To be fair this is scarcely unusual in archaeological history, even where 'professionals' are involved. In 1807 a hoard of nearly 6000 silver pennies of Henry II (1154–89), and dating to the period 1158-80, were found at Tealby in Lincolnshire. The importance of the find was recognized at the time but this did not prevent 5127 being melted down for the silver at the Tower of London and 277 being dispersed amongst collectors. Just twenty were 'reserv'd as a speciment'. The whole affair had been conducted by Sir Joseph Banks (1744–1820), shipmate of James Cook, and President of the Royal Society (Dawson 1999). More recently, the excavation in 1999 of a prehistoric timber monument known as 'Seahenge', on the East Anglian coast, was indeed conducted by professional archaeologists, but in such a manner as to provoke what can only be described as controversy and extremely lively debate.

The plethora of unpublished or delayed excavations, even in modern times, pays witness to the variability of recording even amongst professional academic archaeologists who are swift to criticize others. As a new discipline, aviation archaeology is understandably prone to the kind of mistakes made in other parts of archaeology in earlier times, and which are still being made. It certainly does not do to make undue judgements. As we will see, without the enthusiasm of private input, we would have little to discuss with respect to the archaeological evidence for aircraft of the era, something which applies as much to the conventional archaeology collections of institutions like the British Museum, the Ashmolean in Oxford or the Museum of Antiquities in Newcastle.

Nevertheless, there is a fundamental difference. Aviation archaeology is dealing with the detritus of an extremely well-documented period. As we shall see, it serves a rather different purpose in acting as a channel for the wider population to reach that period and access the intensity and complexity of human experiences which are beyond the wit of even the most conscientious archaeologist to uncover.

2   The historical background

Many books about the Battle of Britain and the Blitz have appeared over the years, from as early as 1941. Most recount in varying amounts of detail the lead-up to the conflict, the day-to-day events and the aftermath as the Battle became the Blitz. They present the evidence in similar form and the result is a fairly consistent presentation of the Battle as a series of defined periods leading to a triumphant outcome, often illustrated by citing a variety of individual experiences. It is also the case that the Battle itself was not well-recorded either with still photography or film. Official sessions were few and far between (**12**), and even fewer pilots had the time or inclination to cart cameras about, with more pressing matters preying on their minds. Consequently, the same small group of images appears repeatedly (and in this book too) while in books on the whole war the episode seems very inconspicuous compared to the monumental record from 1942–5, largely as a result of the entry of the United States into the conflict. The unintentional effect of this is sometimes to isolate the Battle from the rest of the history of the War and to distance the reader from some of the primary evidence.

As this book is as much about the archaeology of the air war it is important to understand how the evidence is distributed, both in time and in the land. The nature of the conflict resulted in an intense rate of air crashes which began over northern France in the spring of 1940, and gravitated across the Channel to southern England before retreating back across the sea once more, as 1940 gave way to 1941. The scale of the air war from 1943 onwards was still beyond the bounds of imagination, but the bulk of this would occur mostly over the continent.

An increasing fascination and horror

Part of understanding the historical image of the Battle of Britain and the Blitz lies in the records of the portentous days of the late 30s. In April 1939 *Reaching for the Stars*, by one Nora Waln, was published, in which she described her years in pre-war Germany. It was reprinted twice within the month, reflecting a growing fascination and apprehension about what might come, and its interest for the British book-buying public. Waln's text contains much admiration for the German people, but a regret that it had come to take on the form it had. She distinguishes the Nazis from the Germans, 'The good in this movement will endure. All other elements the German people will discard'. She found it impossible to believe that the extremities of Nazism could ever appeal beyond a very small portion of the population, perhaps the most interesting observation to an audience benefiting from hindsight. She may have been right but she failed to appreciate the power

*12 Hurricane pilots of No. 32 Squadron at Hawkinge. Left to right they are: P/O R.F. Smythe, P/O K.R. Gillman, P/O J.E. Proctor, F/Lt P.M. Brothers, P/O D.H. Grice, P/O P.M. Gardner, and P/O. A.F. Eckford. The photograph is fortuitously unrepresentative. Gillman (see also **2**) was killed on 25 August 1940 but all the others lived through to the end of the war*

of the Nazis to act out their idiosyncratic dreams.

Waln's views were shared by much of the British public, at least until 1938. There was a profound reluctance to accept the idea that there might be another war with Germany both amongst ordinary people, peers and politicians. Given the appalling experience of the Great War this was entirely understandable; and, of course, there was little appreciation of what Nazism meant for the Jews and other 'racially inferior' groups. The support for appeasement dwindled rapidly once Hitler's territorial ambitions, and his flagrant disregard for agreements, became clear. Parallel with this was a growing terror about the possible consequences of aerial bombardment which we will look at more closely in Chapter 6. But this had major consequences for Britain's preparations (or lack of) for war, dictating the form of the Battle of Britain.

William L. Shirer's *Berlin Diary* did not appear in print until the autumn of 1941, though he had been filing despatches to the American press from there throughout the pre-war period. His private account of the machinations in pre-war Germany, in his own words, recorded his 'increasing fascination and horror' as Europe plunged 'madly down the road to Armageddon'. Unlike Waln he could see clearly what was happening, perhaps because his profession as a journalist meant that the signs were more obvious to him. If they were, they were not plain to all the Germans. On 3 September 1939 Shirer was in the Wilhelmplatz in Berlin when a public announcement was made over the speakers that Britain had declared war on Germany:

> Some 250 people . . . listened attentively to the announcement. When it was finished, there was not a murmur. They just stood as they were before. Stunned. The people cannot realize yet that Hitler has led them into a world war. (Shirer 1941, 161)

Shirer, however, was an American and when the book was sent to the publisher he was still a member of a neutral state. It should never be imagined that the United States' population was somehow unaware of what was going on. Shirer's despatches were amongst many that had kept them informed and there was little suggestion that the USA would be able to ignore the procession of events. She was, in any case, already supplying military hardware to Britain long before formally entering the war in December 1941.

The bomber always gets through

The Battle of Britain would be over who controlled Britain's air space by day. On the outcome depended whether Britain could be freely bombed into submission or not. The change in the character of the air war created a situation in which Britain retained control of her air space by day and gradually came to control air space over Europe. For Germany, it meant a retreat into the night hours which was the only way her bombing campaign could continue. This was despite effectively abandoning any strategic attempt to defeat Britain, and instead it became a retaliatory or punitive response to the Allied effects on her gradually diminishing power and stretched resources. The Allies themselves came to invest spectacular quantities of men and resources in their own day and night bombing campaign over Germany and her occupied territories, reflecting a widely-held conviction that aerial bombardment was a fundamental part of the offensive in modern warfare.

The concept of aerial bombing had developed during the Great War, with Britain the first significant victim. Although these raids were small-scale and arbitrary, involving the use of Zeppelin airships and cumbersome Gotha bomber aircraft, they were regarded as profoundly shocking by the ordinary public. There were 20 Zeppelin raids in 1915 which altogether killed more than 550 people. In 1917 the Gotha bombers replaced them and achieved more devastating results. The daylight raid of 25 May 1917 by 23 Gotha bombers was the first in a series that summer which included 13 June when more than 430 people were killed, including 46 schoolchildren (Terraine 1985, 10).

The German bombers had crossed British territory and acted, to begin with, unchallenged. Once aerial defence had become an issue the Germans started bombing at night. By the end of the Great War, more than 1400 people had been killed. Insignificant though such a total might seem by the standards of the Blitz, the experience for the British public was traumatic and humiliating. It provoked a curious and paradoxical reaction. Bombing, especially of innocent women and children, was regarded with revulsion. But it was also patently clear by the 1920s that some of Britain's potential enemies, which even included France, had the capability to inflict vastly greater civilian losses than had been suffered less than a decade previously. One official estimate suggested a possible daily rate of casualties in a future war of around 850 deaths, and twice that number injured.

The solution was simple enough: do unto the bomber what he plans to do unto you, but do it first and thus prevent him carrying out his intentions. It was also believed that the bomber enjoyed a certain amount of invincibility ('the bomber will always get through', Stanley Baldwin, 1932) and that there was no possibility of conveniently preventing bombing after it had started. In other words, the strategy of the 'knock-out blow' had been transferred from the fields of Flanders, where it had been discredited, up into the air on the basis that things would somehow be different.

This had serious implications for RAF and Air Ministry policy. Fighters, the backbone of air defence, were considered to be low priority and the initiative in their design and development passed by default to private firms and individuals. In any case, political initiative to encourage international disarmament simply foundered when certain countries declined to play ball. Germany's withdrawal from the Disarmament Conference and the League of Nations in 1933 completely undermined the idea that anyone could outlaw bombing, or any other preparations for war for that matter, if one of the participants tore up the rule book. Moreover, many in the military came to believe that pre-emptive large-scale strategic bombing could shorten wars and ultimately help prevent the colossal scale of infantry casualties suffered between 1914 and 1918. Where once the advance of troops was seen as the first line of an offensive, the realization grew that 'the big bombers must be the spearhead of the main attack' (Grey 1941, 1), founded on the theory that destruction of an enemy's resources and infrastructure was fundamental to winning the initiative.

At this distance in time it is still possible to register the scale of the Great War but not perhaps to gauge so easily its impact on politicians, who were utterly determined to prevent a repetition of the trench carnage which, in the inter-war years, was uppermost in almost everyone's mind. While this provoked a widespread policy of appeasement during the rise of fascism it also meant that those who wanted war sought the means to prosecute it with aerial bombardment. In the beginning this led to Germany's Blitzkrieg style of warfare. In the end it led to the comprehensive annihilation of Germany's cities and industrial base once the bombers had reached a size, capacity, and quantity unimaginable in the 1920s.

Before the war broke out scepticism had grown that bombing would be restricted to strategic military targets, and fears that millions of citizens could be killed this way were commonplace. They were fuelled by books such as *Valiant Clay* (1931) by Neil Bell. Bell provided an apprehensive audience with graphic predictions of cities ablaze, citizens 'blown to rags' and survivors gassed. By 1939 this had been given added credibility by the bombing of cities such as Shanghai by Japan in 1932, and Barcelona and Guernica in the Spanish Civil War. German bombing of Warsaw during the fall of Poland showed what

13 The tail section of Heinkel He 111H-4 of 3/KGr126 amongst the ruins of a house in Victoria Avenue in Clacton-on-Sea (Essex). It had been shot down on the night of 30 April 1940 by anti-aircraft fire. The aircraft exploded on crashing, causing the deaths of the crew and two civilians (the first to die as the result of enemy action), and injuring 156 others

might happen to Britain. Not only were the raids widely reported, filmed and photographed, but the arrival of refugees in Britain meant that it was possible to hear firsthand accounts of the destruction of residential areas and the death of ordinary men, women and children.

A nation prepared

When war seemed imminent the reaction in Britain included the evacuation of children, and the provision of air-raid shelters, helpful pamphlets and gas masks. The anticipated devastation simply did not occur, at least to begin with. It was not until 30 April 1940 that the first reported civilian casualties were resulted from an enemy aeroplane. Even then the deaths were caused, not by bombs, but by the shooting-down of a mine-laying Heinkel He 111 which crashed on houses at Clacton (**13**). The reasons were fairly obvious. Until Germany had taken control of Channel airfields it would have been impossible to provide a fighter escort for her bombers over England. Their range and endurance was far too short. Thus the air war in the form and on the scale envisaged in Britain did not even become a possibility until the summer of 1940, explaining further the narrow 'window' in which large numbers of air crashes ended up taking place.

The apparent lack of an 'air war' in 1939 was reflected in contemporary newspapers and books. On 13 October 1939 the Second World War had been underway for around six weeks. Despite this tumultuous event, the *Kentish Mercury* of that day ran a lead story headlined 'Lee man finds Roman relics in his garden'. It shared front-page space with a curiously symbolic story about the collapse of a shop in Deptford which provided some 'unexpected practice' for the suburb's ARP force. Mention of the real war is scarcely apparent, apart from the report that a local woman had been detained by the Gestapo in Germany.

The harsh realities of war had already been brought home for Britain in a rather different theatre by the sinking of the passenger liner *Athenia* on 3 September with the loss of 112 passengers, amongst whom were 28 Americans. In the small hours of the day following the *Kentish Mercury*'s report of Roman revelations in Lee, the battleship *Royal Oak* was destroyed by a U-boat in Scapa Flow. Coming soon after the loss of the carrier HMS *Courageous* this was, as the *Evening News* announced, 'a bad blow for the Navy' in spite of bravely reminding the reader that the new capital ships under construction made the loss of a 23-year-old battleship 'not a crippling blow'.

Considering the fate in store for *Repulse* and *Prince of Wales* a little over two years later off Singapore, the remark indicated the steep learning curve which awaited the navies of all the powers at war as they came to terms with the submarine, and the need to develop carrier-based air power. Only two days later, on 16 October, a German bomber force made an attempt on Britain's most prestigious battleship, HMS *Hood*, in the Firth of Forth. Luck meant *Hood* (some versions say it was *Repulse*) was apparently in dock and, for the time being, German bombing was outlawed on land where civilians might be injured. Other ships were damaged but results included the first German aircraft shot down by Spitfires in action. However positive an experience for Nos. 602 and 603 Squadrons and the men involved, the destruction of two Junkers Ju 88 aircraft scarcely compensated for the loss of *Royal Oak*, which itself followed a series of sinkings by the German pocket battleship *Graf Spee* in the Atlantic.

Nonetheless, much of the record of the period smacks of a kind of complacent satisfaction that Britain's preparations were more than adequate. This was in spite of tirades like 'Cato's' *Guilty Men*, published in July 1940. Appearing in the traumatic aftermath of Dunkirk as the Battle of Britain opened, the text announced that 'This war broke out in 1939. But the genesis of our military misfortunes must be dated at 1929.' (ibid, 17). There follows a castigation of the policy of appeasement and lack of foresight, contrasted with 'clear-eyed and courageous' figures like Churchill. That the little book was reprinted at least eleven times within the month of July 1940 says much for how it impacted on the public mood.

The armed forces had sensed their lack of preparation but a combination of political inertia, military hierarchies, and conservatism conspired to guarantee a potentially disastrous position in early 1940. A group photograph said to have taken at North Weald on 8 October 1939 shows pilots being regaled by Sir Kingsley Wood, then Secretary of State for Air, and Sir John Simon, Chancellor of the Exchequer. The pilots, clad in clean white flying suits with cravats and wearing confident grins, bear a marked contrast with

14   *Sir Kingsley Wood (centre) greets Hurricane pilots of No. 151 Squadron at North Weald on 8 October 1939. The image contrasts greatly with those of pilots a year later*

images of their exhausted counterparts slumped over seats a year later. More than that, behind these smiling young men, whose smiles would soon be wiped off their faces, is one of their magnificent flying machines replete with fixed-pitch, two-bladed, propeller (**14**).

The two-bladed propeller was to prove inadequate in the early air battles to come, initially depriving both Hurricanes and Spitfires of potential speed and rate of climb (**15**). In this respect it symbolized the failure to appreciate immediately Germany's development of a huge modern airforce. During the Battle of France the following spring, Paul Richey of No. 1 Squadron (**4**) would experience for himself the transformation of the unit's Hurricanes when the propellers were replaced with three-bladed, two-pitch, and then variable pitch, versions. However, this deficiency seems scarcely worth mentioning when one considers that in the summer of 1939 an Air Ministry minute was able to announce that as 'Merlin IIIs [the engine fitted to Spitfires and Hurricanes] are required for foreign orders', Spitfires due for delivery between November 1939 and March 1940 'should be delivered without engines' (cited in MS, 50). Considering that the Merlin III represented one of the pinnacles of British aviation engine development at the time, it seems quite beyond belief that foreign air forces were to be given priority in its acquisition.

Richey and his colleagues at least enjoyed the use of guns and radios. No. 92 Squadron was equipped with twin-engined Bristol Blenheims in the winter of 1939–40 which, at the time, were fitted with neither. The problem was not cost or design, simply that the hardware did not exist in sufficient numbers. The aircraft themselves may have been state

15   *The pilots of No. 1 Squadron stage a posed scramble in France in the winter of 1939/40. The Hurricane nearest the camera has the fixed-pitch twin-bladed propeller, which was to prove so inadequate in the months to come. The second Hurricane has been equipped with a variable pitch three-bladed version which was vastly more effective*

of the art for the British aviation industry in the mid-30s. By 1940 they were already too slow and poorly-armed to serve as adequate fighters. The problem was compounded by the command structure of the RAF which, unavoidably to begin with, placed men with no combat experience in charge of men who were rapidly accumulating a lifetime's experience of frontline warfare in a few days. Brian Kingcome, who flew with Nos. 65 and 92 Squadrons during 1940 recalled a 'time warp in which COs of front-line squadrons were selected on a basis of age and length of service rather than operational experience and ability' (Kingcome 1999, 95). This was at a time when German units were led, and manned, by men who had fought in the Spanish Civil War.

The RAF pilots themselves were keen, but many had exceedingly little experience on the machines they were flying in combat. In September 1938 just one, untrained, squadron (No. 19) was even partially equipped with Spitfires. Training accidents were common and even once operational, other problems came rapidly into play. In the early part of the war some of the enthusiastic pilots were having difficulty with aircraft recognition, anticipating the pot-shots to be taken at Spitfires and Hurricanes over Dunkirk by terrified British soldiers. On 6 September 1939 in the early morning, Hurricanes from Nos. 56 and 151 Squadrons at North Weald (Essex), and Spitfires from Nos. 54, 65, and 74 Squadrons at Hornchurch (Essex) were scrambled to meet aircraft which had been spotted over the Thames Estuary. Unfortunately, a combination of disorganization and inexperience led the two groups to attack one another. In the melee a Hurricane pilot, Montagu Hulton-Harrap, was killed and the occasion has since become known as the Battle of Barking Creek. On 28 October 1939 F/Lt Hodge of No. 602 Squadron 'sighted ANSON [a British aircraft] which I mistook for [an] E(nemy) A(ircraft). I then put section [A] into line astern and attacked. Having given [a] short burst [of machine gun fire] I realized [my] mistake.' This bald and heavily-abbreviated account seems to suggest the Anson and its crew survived intact to fight another day. It was just as well that until Germany took control of airfields in northern France there would be no significant chance of a major air conflict over Britain.

Perfecting the lines of defence

As the pilots of Fighter Command gradually came to terms with what awaited them, the British Expeditionary Force had established itself amongst the French and Belgian forces facing the expected German invasion. There was little sensation of panic. The conquest of Poland which occasioned Britain's abandonment of appeasement was regarded with a scandalized detachment by the British public. The prospect of a revisitation of the Western Front was regarded with official confidence. Churchill announced on 9 January 1940, while visiting the vanguard, that 'anyone at home who feels a bit gloomy or fretful about the war would benefit very much by spending a few days with the French and British Armies.'

Skene Catling's *Vanguard to Victory* appeared in early 1940. Subtitled 'An account of the first months of the British Expeditionary Force in France', it stands as a remarkable artefact of the period in its own right. Considering that it can hardly have been sold for many weeks before the horror of Blitzkrieg came upon the allied forces, the book must have seemed horribly ill-timed to the superstitious as the year wore on. 'Perfecting the lines of defence', the army is presented as a model of discipline and organization, visited by the King and members of the government. A contemporary account by one of the soldiers recounted (albeit with the benefit of hindsight), that even when German reconnaissance increased in the spring 'no word came to us to expect trouble. We just continued on our boring way' (Irwin 1943, 28).

The 26 April 1940 edition of *War Illustrated* magazine anticipated 'the great clash, which may come at any moment' but confidently informed the reader that Germany was producing 'freak guns . . . of doubtful military value'. Posed photographs of poised Allied troops in France followed, but the main thrust of the edition was to cover the fall of

Norway, and the arrival of another British expeditionary force there to confront the Germans. At this stage though, British naval supremacy was still considered the decisive factor. It still seemed that way. German losses in the two sea battles of Narvik were sufficient to inhibit her capacity either to invade Britain or break out into the high seas. But by mid-1940 the Battle of the Atlantic was underway and, with the sinking of HMS *Glorious* and her complement of aircraft being brought home from the campaign in Norway, Britain's vulnerability was apparent to all. After centuries of confident reliance on the supremacy of the Royal Navy the susceptibility of capital ships to a form of warfare still barely a generation old, which would reach its climax at Midway in 1942 in the Pacific, would be a bitter pill to swallow.

In the meantime, *War Illustrated* reported that France's premier, Paul Reynaud, believed the Allied forces would be decisive on land too. The magazine shared Reynaud's confidence and in the edition of 10 May highlighted how 'Nazi parachutists dropped to death in Norway'. Scarcely a mention is made of the Low Countries and France's borders because the magazine's editors, like everyone else except the Germans, believed the Maginot Line was impregnable. The outcome in Norway was that the Allies were withdrawn and on 9 June the Norwegian army surrendered. The Prime Minister, Neville Chamberlain, had been forced to resign on 9 May more or less directly as a result of the Norwegian campaign happening at all.

A sudden change in fortune

Walter Lord's vivid account of the impending débâcle in France, assembled from innumerable eyewitness accounts, includes a marvellous piece of understatement about the consequences of 10 May 1940. On that day the German advance west commenced and 'most of the BEF were . . . mystified by the sudden change in fortune' (Lord 1982, 6). A freezing winter of billets and a mixture of French bonhomie and outright belligerence (the British were often blamed for the war) had created a kind of convenient routine. British soldiers became accustomed to their enforced and static exile in which drills and preparation of defences went literally hand-in-hand with the local farmer's or innkeeper's daughter.

The arrival of Panzer tanks, motorcycles, and swarms of Messerschmitts, Dorniers, and Heinkels, had been anticipated but, despite the experiences of Poland and Norway, no-one seemed to have that much expectation of what total war would involve (**16**). There was, quite literally, a disbelieving paralysis to begin with. Even taking into account the level of training the soldiers had received, it had not included confronting high-speed tank advances accompanied by dive-bombers. Dealing with this meant air power and there had scarcely been time between September 1939 and May 1940 to develop it.

The transition from passive defence to blistering retreat was as traumatic as it was abrupt. All the assumptions, if not presumptions, about the course of the war were destroyed in the space of a little over three weeks, beginning on 10 May 1940. No. 92 Squadron was one of several units summoned to help defend the allied forces in France (**17**). Although made up of well-trained regulars, as opposed to volunteer reservists, the

16 *The Junkers Ju 87 (Stuka) in flight. The non-retractable undercarriage and minimal defensive armament were not relevant when used in surprise attacks against civilian targets like Polish towns. Their terrifying sound (caused by special devices fitted under the wings) disoriented victims and witnesses alike. Against RAF fighters the Stuka proved an easy target especially while exposing their bellies in dive-bombing attacks (**10**). The type was soon withdrawn from the west*

17 *Spitfire I, P9372 GR-G, of No. 92 Squadron around the time of the Battle of France while the unit's machines still bore the GR code (after June 1940 it was QJ). This aircraft was destroyed on 9 September 1940. (Allan Wright)*

pilots had nonetheless no combat experience at all, unlike their putative foes. They arrived at Hornchurch on 22 May, to begin the following morning a brief and bloody introduction to the shape of things to come. Sent to patrol over Boulogne, four of No. 92's twelve Spitfires were lost before the day was out. One of the pilots lost was their squadron leader, Roger Bushell, later to be immortalized as the Roger Bartlett of the celebrated feature film of the book called *The Great Escape*. Bushell had survived, later to be murdered by the Germans, but two of the others were dead. Nearly sixty years later, Allan Wright, another pilot with the squadron, recalled how shocked he and his colleagues were when Bushell was lost, though the experience seems to have concentrated their minds on the job in hand:

> We felt leaderless. But [Roger] had taught us well, led us and inspired us; summarized in our battle cry 'Fight or be killed'. Despite the loss of our leader on our very first day in action we continued to shoot down enemy aircraft over Dunkirk at a higher rate than most others. (A.R. Wright, to the author, 1999)

To the soldiers on the ground — fighting with their backs to the wall all the way to the beach and, if they were lucky, out to sea to be rescued and taken home — the chance to participate in an aerial battle must have seemed like luxury. There was considerable resentment caused by the long periods when air cover was apparently absent, and then by the fact that the squadrons could not be seen at high altitude. In the interludes, and at lower altitudes, the Luftwaffe was able freely to strafe and bomb the chaotic mass of men and ships below. In fact, during the nine days of the operation at Dunkirk, the RAF flew thousands of sorties, losing 99 fighters (including 42 Spitfires) and 46 other types (Terraine 1985, 157). It was a painful introduction to the air war (see Chapter 4).

The outcome of Dunkirk is well known and needs no retelling here. The important point for us is that it simplified the situation by closing off all military options and isolated Britain from the continent. The pre-war fantasy of a knock-out blow led by bombers was displaced. Germany's control of French Channel airfields made the air war over Britain an actual possibility. Now the fighters would have their day and the nature of the conflict would be dictated by the efforts of the pilots and the workers at Hawkers and Vickers-Supermarine, the archaeological consequences of which we shall explore later.

Nature of the Battle

Unlike most battles, the Battle of Britain lasted for several months, from 10 July to 31 October 1940. These dates are rather arbitrary and have the effect of creating an illusion that there was a grand opening, a climax and an end in which the survivors, bloodied but unbowed, tramped across the battlefield to gather the glorious dead. The idea of a 'battle' also seems superficially dubious. In fact, it is entirely appropriate. At even a low altitude of around 2000ft in a light aircraft above the middle of Kent it is easy to see from London to Dover, and Essex to Sussex, all at once. All the principal towns and routes of south-east England are easily visible, laid out almost like a board game. To men flying machines which were capable of crossing this area in minutes (a Spitfire could fly from Biggin Hill to Dover in less than a quarter of an hour) it was exactly like moving across a battlefield with its patches of high ground, low ground, valleys and rivers. Not only that, but even today many of the wartime fighter airfields can still be picked out with ease. All these features guided the Luftwaffe in, and were the clues by which the RAF men found their ways home, or suitable fields in which to force-land.

Nonetheless, the very definition of chronological parameters, almost by force of circumstance, begs the historian to create (and dispute) a formal set of events, strategies, and tactics. The considerable number of books on the period reflects this. But the outcome of the Battle of Britain, as with so many battles, had already been to a large extent decided. As we shall see, German over-confidence, preparations and tactics, the limitations of their fighters, and the very nature of an air war where bombers, the lumbering elephants of an offensive campaign, were set against highly-motivated fighter pilots using machines that were utilized to their best advantage, made the end something of a foregone conclusion.

The reality was that the perception at the time was somewhat more diffuse, though there was an acute sense of occasion. Few of the participants saw continuous action throughout the period. The movement of squadrons, injuries, and death put paid to the chances of many of seeing it through. Richard Hillary (**5**), for example, the celebrated author of *The Last Enemy* (1942), was in action for little more than a week before appalling burns confined him to hospital. What therefore is presented in books in the form of graphical reconstructions of days in the battle was, for many of the participants, a few blistering confrontations in the air conducted at breakneck speed over places which were temporarily unrecognizable. Flaked out by physical and emotional exhaustion few of these men, pilots and mechanics alike, had (at the time) much sense of a neat progression of events and nor would it have mattered to them anyway.

The German plan to invade Britain was real enough, enshrined in the preparations of a fleet in the Channel ports for 'Operation Sealion', though it was not what Hitler had wanted. From the outset he had fantasized about making a peace with Britain, a country which he admired. Britain's refusal to play this game led to his plan 'to eliminate the English motherland as a base from which war against Germany can be continued, and, if necessary, to occupy completely' (Hitler's Directive no. 16, cited by Terraine 1985, 173). The accumulating invasion fleet remained at anchor in French ports while an aerial battle proceeded in a manner which at the time must have resembled attrition. The Luftwaffe sent waves of aircraft over the Channel, initially charged with the destruction of Britain's shipping (**24**), then moved inland to assault RAF bases, aerial defences and radar systems, and finally altered tactics to attacking her cities. The transference of the Luftwaffe's attention to London altered the character of the aerial battle. The Battle of Britain was eventually transformed into the night bombing of the Blitz, aircraft losses on both sides fell, and the daylight air war moved over the Channel once more and back to the continent.

The British had little immediate need for bombers in such circumstances, though they existed and were in regular use with variable success. But RAF bombers did not play an integral part in the daily conflicts that made up the Battle of Britain. RAF fighters, mostly single-engined monoplanes, fought above home territory and only occasionally beyond. Dowding's reluctance to release his precious Spitfires for duties during the fall of France was vindicated, the experiences of Nos. 74 and 92 Squadrons illustrating what could have happened during longer exposure.

Losses

In operating an offensive campaign it was necessary for the Luftwaffe to draw the RAF fighters into the sky and destroy them faster than they could be replaced. The purpose was to crush effective aerial opposition to an invading force. The lack of British ground forces and equipment meant that any reciprocal Allied invasion of France was totally out of the question. Therefore, to pick a fight, German aircraft had to fly across the Channel and over England.

This instantly put the German fighter pilots at a huge disadvantage. The Messerschmitt Bf 109 (**20**) had a fuel capacity of only 88 gallons. Despite its superior armament and fuel-injection engine, much of its flying time was occupied in getting to England and back. It could not fly beyond the London area and at best could afford only about twenty minutes combat time. The twin-engined Messerschmitt Bf 110 made good this deficiency (it carried about three times as much fuel) but its cumbersome handling meant the aircraft became outclassed in a dogfight once RAF pilots had the measure of it (**18**). It was also the case that the RAF had developed an organized form of aerial warfare based on radar. Despite the problems with the systems and interpreting the results, the overall effect was that RAF fighters were normally sent into the air only when and where needed, thus avoiding wasting resources and making sure that fully-armed and fuelled machines greeted Luftwaffe aircraft which were already counting the minutes before turning for home. The overall consequence was that fighting took place mainly over south-east England or the sea and each occasion was extremely brief. It has been said that, despite these disadvantages, the sheer numbers of German aircraft combined with the experience of their pilots and their more flexible tactics led to initial successes for the Luftwaffe.

This was certainly true in a fighter-for-fighter calculation but overall the figures look less alarming. On 11 July 1940 for example, 11 Spitfires and Hurricanes were downed, six of which were repairable. A single Blenheim was damaged but that too was repairable. The net RAF loss for the day was five aircraft. On 14 July the figures were one Hurricane lost and one repairable. In contrast, on 11 July although no Messerschmitt 109s were lost, the Luftwaffe lost at least 16 other aircraft, with several others returning to base damaged. On 14 July the Luftwaffe lost three aircraft, with a further three damaged. On 17 July the RAF lost only one machine (four others were repairable), and even that was for unknown reasons. Only one of the repairable machines had been damaged by a German fighter. The Luftwaffe conversely lost four bombers, with a fifth repairable. None of these was directly attributable to the RAF but the fact remains that Fighter Command's net loss was one, and the Luftwaffe's four.

There are various practical implications of this pattern. What mattered either to the

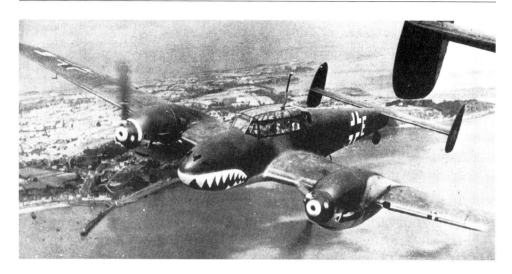

18 *Messerschmitt Bf 110 on patrol. It proved cumbersome in dogfights with Spitfires and Hurricanes*

RAF or the Luftwaffe was the capacity to replace losses, both machines and men, on a daily basis however good or bad that day had been. Thus a loss of five aircraft but an ability to replace only three is vastly more dangerous than a loss of 100 combined with an ability instantly to provide 110 replacements. For Britain, being able to sustain losses meant retaining control of her sky and thus either prevent an invasion or bombing from overwhelming the nation's ability to resist capitulation. For Germany, replacing losses was fundamental to prosecuting an offensive war.

Not surprisingly, it is not very easy to assess what the situation was for either side. The instinctive British tendency to focus on the most dramatic phase of the Battle perhaps makes things look worse, and therefore the results more impressive, than they really were. Throughout August and the first half of September, British losses certainly exceeded the rate of production. The difference was made good on a make-do-and-mend basis in various ways. More than four-thousand aircraft were repaired and returned to service in the second half of 1940; obviously many went through the system several times). Reserve machines were used, and so were the resources of the Fighter Groups based away from the heart of the Battle (Hough and Richards 1990, 249). Obviously, this could not be sustained indefinitely but anticipating such an outcome presupposes that the circumstances causing such losses could have been sustained themselves, and that the rate of replacement might not be improved.

In fact, during the periods before and after the climactic six weeks of August and early September, British fighter production generally exceeded losses. The record cards of some machines, such as Hurricane I, Z7010, show they sat out the Battle as reserves in RAF Maintenance Units and were never required. The change in fortune from late September is partly attributable to the fall in losses as German attention was gradually transferred to night bombing of cities.

19 RAF Bomber Command crews pose with a Vickers Wellington bomber to celebrate the RAF's first bombing of Berlin

The critical factor was that Germany could not sustain the situation herself. Meanwhile, for Britain, things were improving. Manufacture of Hurricanes in Canada had begun (of which Z7010 was one) and the new Spitfire factory at Castle Bromwich went into production. This produced the Spitfire Mark II, a faster version of the Mark I, which started to reach frontline squadrons in August. As we shall see, taken over the whole period, the figures for Britain are much better than is usually implied by books on the period.

The change in German strategy is normally considered to be the defining moment in the Battle. It followed RAF Bomber Command raids on Berlin on 25/26 August, which left Berliners stunned with disbelief and the German high command incandescent with rage and embarrassment (Hermann Göring, commander of the Luftwaffe, had promised this would never happen). Shirer thought the anti-aircraft fire 'magnificent, a terrible sight' and watched as the 'naïve and simple' Berliners who had believed Göring fled in a 'frightened rush for the shelters' (1941, 381). On the night of 28/29 August the RAF came back over Berlin (**19**).

This led to the ending of daylight attacks on RAF bases as the Luftwaffe began revenge bombing of German cities. But to claim this new strategy changed everything presupposes that, had the Germans not changed their strategy, they would inevitably have overwhelmed Fighter Command through sheer weight of numbers. The Luftwaffe had begun with considerably more aircraft than the RAF, but was also losing them at as high or higher a rate. Hough and Richards state that between mid-August and mid-September the Luftwaffe lost 467 bombers, 'just over one-sixth of its operational strength' (op. cit., 247).

One source (Shepherd 1975) says that German fighter production in June and July 1940 at 164 and just over 200 respectively, was barely half that of Britain's in the same period. Another source (Deighton 1980, 165), dealing with single-engined fighter production only, states that German monthly fighter production averaged 156 in 1940 while Britain produced a mean of 370 monthly in 1940, a result achieved by elevating average monthly production from 155 in the first quarter of 1940 to 563 and 420 in the third and fourth quarters respectively). As early as April 1940 actual production of fighters was exceeding planned production. In August 282 were planned, and 476 turned out (Terraine 1985, 191). If Britain was generating more new machines than Germany to replenish what had been a smaller stockpile to begin with then it is plain enough that Britain's *rate* of replacement was better than Germany's. It means that Germany would get into trouble faster. Although she had more to begin with, she was fielding more daily and losing them at a higher rate than Britain. A large bath with a large drain hole and replenished only by a trickle will empty faster than a small bath with a small drain hole replenished by a steady flow. The result, as observed by Michael Bowyer in a recent survey of aircraft in use by the RAF in 1940, was a 'Fighter Command remarkably intact at the end of its gruelling fight (1991, 13).

Perhaps more importantly, each German bomber, plus the Messerschmitt Bf 110 fighter, lost meant the German armaments industry lost two engines (except the Stuka), and cost the Luftwaffe from two to five trained (and in the early stage, experienced) men. The British Defiant and Blenheim had crews of two and three respectively but they constituted such a small minority of RAF fighters involved in the Battle that the point is not affected. That mattered hugely in 1940. The nature of loss changed for the Luftwaffe as the conflict drifted over the English mainland with the alteration in German tactics during the late summer of 1940; now the numbers of men who could be recovered from the sea by a highly-efficient sea rescue service diminished. The RAF was also affected, but for the better. This is notwithstanding the losses that RAF Bomber Command was beginning to incur in its raids over the continent and accidents in Britain, but here we are concerned specifically with what fighting the Battle of Britain was costing each side.

It seems impossible to avoid the conclusion that it was extremely expensive for Germany, whose military planners had never prepared their armaments industry for such losses and, as the war went against them, were denied the opportunity to remedy the shortcomings. In any case, despite RAF Bomber Command's losses, their actual number of aircraft was relatively small at this time. In mid-July 1940 Bomber Command had 575 aircraft, including reserves, while Fighter Command had 1418 including reserves (Townshend Bickers 1990, 64 and 85). By way of comparison, Fighter Command's losses to 18 August were over 200, while Bomber Command's losses on raids that were designed to prevent the invasion were about 18 (Terraine 1985, 189).

As the air war moved more into the skies over Kent and Sussex during August, British pilots whose machines were badly damaged but had themselves survived could either attempt emergency landings or bale out, eventually to get back to base by car or, in what seems an extraordinarily prosaic way to return to the most famous frontline in British history, public transport. Richard Hillary, shot down for the first time on 29 August, parachuted into a field near Lympne only to find a colleague, Colin Pinckney, suspended

*20 Messerschmitt Bf 109E-3 (4101) of 2/JG51 at Hendon. This aircraft saw service in the Battle of Britain before being converted to a fighter-bomber role. On 27 November 1940 Lt Wolfgang Teumer made a force-landing at Manston (Kent) after the engine's cooling system was damaged by fire from Spitfires. On 14 December the machine was delivered to Rolls-Royce, later being transferred to the Aircraft and Armament Experimental Establishment at Boscombe Down. It is an exceptionally rare and intact survivor of the Luftwaffe from the period. See also **colour plate 9***

by his parachute from a tree, having been shot down moments earlier. Hillary arrived back at No. 603 Squadron's base the following afternoon and Pinckney a while later once minor burn wounds had been treated (Hillary 1942, 133). Peter Olver, shot down on his first sortie on 25 October 1940, returned to No. 603 at Hornchurch on the London Underground clutching his parachute and nursing a head injury (**colour plate 6**). Such experiences taught harsh lessons, but meant that wiser pilots returned to the fray and helped sustain experienced manpower resources. It was also RAF policy to withdraw badly-mauled or exhausted squadrons from the frontline. For example, No. 54 Squadron played an active role in the skies over Dunkirk and the first part of the Battle of Britain. On 3 September it was pulled out, returning to the frontline in 1941. This policy helped preserve experienced pilots such as Alan Deere who were either able to offer their skills in later combat or in training new pilots.

Surviving German pilots shot down in similar confrontations found themselves in prison and withdrawn from the war, while those who made it home were obliged to continue the fight almost without respite usually until they were killed themselves. One of many examples was Oblt Bartels, shot down in his Bf 109 on 24 July 1940 near Margate.

21 Messerschmitt Bf 110D (Wk no. 3338) S9+CK of Stab ErpGr 210 being prepared for public display at Hendon. This seems to correspond with records of a Bf 110 which came down on 15 August 1940 at Bletchingly Farm, Catts Hill, Rotherfield (Kent)

Seriously wounded, the war for him was over and he was imprisoned (**20**). Where a bomber was concerned, the loss of manpower was even more serious. Late at night on 29 August 1940 a Heinkel He 111 of 3/KG27 was shot down near Bristol. The crew of four were all captured, though one later died of his injuries.

For essentially the same reasons, repairable British aircraft were sent off to be mended whereas German aircraft were left where they fell, went to the melting pot, or were put on public display for fundraising (**21**). Overall, on 29 August combat and routine accidents cost Fighter Command 14 aircraft, four of which were repairable, but 12 of whose pilots survived in British hands. Some were injured but all were capable of returning to their units immediately or within a few weeks. The Luftwaffe, on the other hand, lost 33 aircraft that day also to combat and routine accidents, nine of which were badly damaged. At least 16 of the pilots were killed, plus around two to three times that number of additional crew members. Two pilots were captured in Britain.

Taken over the period in total, losses estimated for the Battle of Britain vary from source to source. Some degree of comparison is available from figures compiled by *After the Battle* Magazine for their outstanding book *The Battle of Britain, Then and Now* (1989, 707). In summary these state the losses for the RAF and Luftwaffe between 10 July and 31 October to have been:

July 10-31	Aircrew	Aircraft
RAF	68	91
Luftwaffe	348	185
August		
RAF	176	389
Luftwaffe	993	694
September		
RAF	173	358
Luftwaffe	829	629
October		
RAF	120	185
Luftwaffe	492	379

Total losses	RAF	Luftwaffe
Aircrew	537	2662
Aircraft	1023	1887

The totals speak for themselves but they can be looked at in several different ways. Firstly, the Luftwaffe lost around five times as many men as the RAF in the Battle of Britain. This bears out the point that the majority of German aircraft lost cost the Luftwaffe between two and five men, and that surviving RAF crew were more likely to bale out over friendly territory.

Secondly, the Luftwaffe lost about 1.8 times as many aircraft as the RAF. This conceals the fact that only around one third of these were single-engined aircraft. If we estimate that 1200 twin-engined machines were involved, that leaves us with about 3000 engines lost, or *three times* as many as the RAF (**22**).

A point almost never made, if at all, is that the Luftwaffe engines were in many respects more mechanically sophisticated and thus more difficult to make than the Rolls-Royce Merlin, despite the plaudits heaped on the latter. A couple of simple examples will illustrate this. The Merlin valve rockers were solid cast items, with a hardened pad for the camshaft to strike. Each of the four rows of twelve-valve rockers pivoted on a common shaft. The Jumo 211, fitted for example to the Junkers Ju 88, had exhaust valve rockers which pivoted on individual shafts with a sleeved bronze bush and, instead of having an integral hardened pad, had a roller pad rotating on its own threaded shaft inserted into the rocker (**colour plate 22**). This made repairs and maintenance easier but manufacture involved more parts, machined to higher tolerances.

The Daimler-Benz engine, fitted to the Bf 109 and 110 for example, had extremely heavy-duty roller bearings on its crankshaft. Without going into the arcane details of engine manufacture, what this amounted to was a reliable and strong method where the load was carried by rotating bearings packed around the moving parts (incidentally, factories manufacturing these bearings were considered so important that they were the

22 *Dornier Do 17Z-3 (Wk no. 2669) of 4/KG3. The aircraft raided Hornchurch on 31 August 1940 (**67**) but was damaged by ground fire during the raid and on its way home. The machine crashed on the shore off Sandwich (Kent) where it was set on fire by the crew (who were all taken prisoner). The crumbling ash of the fuselage flanked by the engines illustrates how the physical form of the aircraft could be reduced to almost nothing. The aircraft's remains are reputed to be visible at low tide to this day*

target of US bombers in the disastrous Schweinfurt raids of August and October 1943 — see Epilogue). In the Rolls-Royce Merlin plain bearings were used, relying exclusively on oil pressure to keep the parts separated enough to prevent seizure and failure. Like the Jumo rockers, the Daimler-Benz crankshaft was far more complicated than the Rolls-Royce equivalent

In other words, to stay in the fight on an even keel the Luftwaffe was having to field up to five times as many men, and between twice and three times as much equipment which was itself often much more difficult and costly to make. Admirable though the quality of German aircraft manufacture was, and this is often evident even from wrecked motors, it was an inefficient process of making war. By 1945 the winners were those who could turn out war *materiel* in vast quantities. There was no point in wasting resources on building machines to last which were only going to serve for hours or days. Not only that, but large quantities of resources were being poured into preparing the invasion fleet. Many of the barges were fitted with aircraft engines, fitted with propellers in the manner of a hovercraft. This meant further diversion of aviation resources.

Another way of looking at the figures is to compare fighters against fighters but this is fairly meaningless. The Battle of Britain conflict involved pitching British fighters against

German fighters and bombers. This is what was fielded on the day. It would be equally meaningless to assess losses at Agincourt in 1415 only by comparing English archer losses against French archers, and omitting the French losses of armoured knights.

Today it is 15 September which is celebrated as 'Battle of Britain Day'. This is partly thanks to its very approximate midway position in the recognized period of the Battle, and because two days later Hitler postponed any attempt to invade Britain. After the day in question the claimed victories over German aircraft were '188 certain, 45 probable, 78 damaged', though exact figures varied in newspapers the following morning. The results seemed to be especially successful and attributable to the regrouping and re-equipping of squadrons. The participation of the so-called 'Big Wing' from Duxford, which involved five squadrons in massed formation confronting the German bombers heightened the perceived significance of the day.

The occasion is a good illustration of the inadequacy of immediate contemporary records, though problems in interpreting them have already been described. Several pilots claiming a victory over the same machine were unwittingly responsible and the authorities were only too happy to accommodate over-estimates. The products were headlines like those of the *Daily Express* on 16 September announcing, '175 Shot Down ... all the way from the coast to London the countryside is strewn with the wreckage of shot down Nazi fighters.' *Express* readers were informed that the triumphant victories had been won at a cost of 30 RAF fighters, ten of whose pilots had been recovered. Colin Perry recorded his version of the day's results in his diary for 16 September: 'we shot down 189 planes yesterday. We only lost 25 fighters. Magnificent' (Perry 1972).

The reconstruction of the day's events has generally involved substantially reducing the Luftwaffe losses by ruling out duplicate claims and tying them into actual crashes as well as Luftwaffe records. Nonetheless, the myth of a 'dramatic victory' for the RAF that day has been sustained, being described as such in a 1999 television series on the period called *Their Finest Hour*, apparently as the result of a completely uncritical acceptance of newspapers headlines from nearly 60 years earlier. Reducing the figures certainly seems to qualify the RAF's achievements that day. But if we consider the factors outlined above, 15 September still turns out to have been an expensive day for the Luftwaffe. In fact, the Luftwaffe is now known on 15 September to have lost around 60 machines, with a further 23 making it home despite being damaged. The RAF lost about 30. Post-war examination of Luftwaffe and RAF records, tied up with excavations of machines make this an approximate certainty.

The point of course is that the figures provided at the time on a daily basis were psychologically essential and, oddly, perhaps still are. Had the British public appreciated the game of stalemate that was being played out in the skies above, the mood of resilient optimism might have been less easily sustained though things were not as bad as the true figures for 15 September suggest. The corrected figures for 15 September show that Luftwaffe aircraft losses were about double the RAF's, and therefore very close to the average for the whole period. Of the 60, 25 were single-engined Bf 109s. Thus the day cost the Luftwaffe 95 engines, the RAF 31, or one-third. RAF aircrew lost on 15 September were 16, while the Luftwaffe lost over 90. At nearly 1:6 this was worse than the average for Luftwaffe aircrew losses over the period.

The end of daylight bombing

It is plain that the Germans could not have sustained their daylight efforts over south-east England indefinitely. If this had become obvious enough to the German High Command by the middle of September, it was obvious to other people too, as William L. Shirer observed,

> It's a fact that since about a fortnight the Germans have given up large-scale day attacks on England and have gone over largely to night bombing. This in itself is an admission of defeat.
> (Shirer 1941, 405, Berlin, 23 September 1940)

In other words, it had become impossible, quite quickly, for Germany to sustain her own losses. She did not have the preparations or resources to do so, simply because the nature of the Battle of Britain and its duration had not been anticipated by her leaders. This was demoralizing for the Luftwaffe pilots whose only reward was to be castigated by their commander-in-chief, Göring, for a lack of fighting spirit. His solution was to order more large-scale attacks which provided more trade, in the parlance of the squadron operations room, for Fighter Command.

Therefore the perceived danger of Britain's short-term reliance on reserve aircraft is entirely academic. If Germany was to maintain a campaign against Britain a move to night bombing was inevitable, given the losses. This was what happened in the Great War. German daylight bombing was abandoned after August 1917 once British defences were mobilized and replaced with night attacks which were kept up until the following May. RAF Bomber Command was also to find that daylight losses were so catastrophic they could not be sustained. In the context of the later air war, daylight bombing of Germany by the USAAF between 1942 and 1945 was only sustainable for two reasons. Firstly, US industrial production and manpower was so overwhelming that enormous losses were (just) sustainable, though for a time even this seemed touch and go. Secondly, the production of the long-range P-51 Mustang fighter completely altered the 'traditional' bombing scenario in which the bomber was left exposed to attacks by the defenders' fighters as their own fighter escort, short of fuel, peeled off for home. This had allowed the German defenders the same advantages enjoyed by Fighter Command in 1940 of recovering their pilots who were only conducting relatively short-range missions. The Mustang altered all that by being able to escort bombers deep into the heart of Germany, protecting them, and accompanying them all the way home.

Back in 1940, had the Germans been equipped with a fighter which had a comparable range to its bombers, then the outcome of the Battle of Britain might have been very different. This is a favourite topic of speculation amongst historians of the Battle but is as pointless as saying, had the Germans been equipped in 1940 with a long-range, high-powered faster-than-sound, and heavily-armed, jet fighter then she might have won. The fact is she was not. Moreover, her production capacity at the time could never conceivably have matched her losses. The climax of the Battle of Britain lasted no longer than it took for this to become clear. This is not in any sense to diminish the courage and fortitude exhibited at the time (**23**). Britain's achievement was to stay in the fight and cause Germany unsustainable losses that provoked a change of strategy, fundamental to which was the recognition that invasion was impossible.

Shirer recorded the admiration which he heard at firsthand from a member of Luftwaffe, 'the German pilots have the highest admiration for their British adversaries — for their skill and bravery' (ibid., 404). In 1941 he compiled some retrospective comments to insert in the publication of his *Berlin Diary* later that year. As an observation this passage is remarkable in an analysis which has been repeatedly 'rediscovered' by later historians of the period:

> I think the truth is that while the British never risked more than a small portion of their available fighters on any one day, they did send up enough to destroy more German bombers per day than Göring could afford to lose . . . These were blows which made the Luftwaffe momentarily groggy and which it could not indefinitely sustain despite its numerical superiority, because the British were losing only a third or fourth as many planes, though, to be sure, they were mostly fighters. (Shirer 1941, 435-6)

Shirer had no access to the true figures of losses, nor could he have done, but this does not affect the point that German failure in the sky over Britain in 1940 could be seen as having been more or less obviously inevitable by 1941 given the loss rates, the replacement rates, and the tactics. For the archaeological context, the implications are different. The overall figures summarized above indicate that more crash sites of German aircraft occurred, and that more German engines or remains of aircrew ought to be recoverable from the ground. Moreover, as RAF machines were more likely to be recovered for reuse, there is perhaps even less chance of locating an RAF machine. Spitfire I, N3119, of No. 222 Squadron was shot down on 30 October 1940. It was recovered, repaired, and reused until 1942. Examination of its 1940 crash site yielded only fragments. In any case RAF crash sites have been more assiduously searched for and therefore the figures of sites explored do not reflect the proportions of actual losses. However, the pattern of fighting dictates a geographical distribution which varies through the period of the Battle, also affected by contemporary recovery.

During July 1940, most of the Luftwaffe's activity was concentrated on attacking Channel shipping (**24**). On 14 July the principal target, for example, had been a convoy off Dover. Consequently, the losses incurred were usually over water and are thus effectively excluded (normally) from the available archaeological record. They subsist only in the documentary record. This included the single net loss to the RAF that day. Hurricane I, L1584, of No. 615 Squadron fell into St. Margaret's Bay, where presumably it still is. The pilot, P/O M.R. Mudie, was rescued but died later.

As German strategy altered to executing attacks on RAF bases during August so the accessible record starts to increase, though even then it normally constitutes a small proportion of what actually occurred. The events of 18 August involved devastating Luftwaffe assaults on, for example, Tangmere and Kenley. A proportion of crashed aircraft from the day have been examined, both British and German. Even so, the vast majority of

23 *The tail section of Dornier Do 17Z (Wk no. 2361) of 1/KG76 lying on the roof of a building in Vauxhall Bridge. The aircraft broke up when it was shot down over Victoria at 1150 on 15 September 1940 in a dogfight involving at least six British fighters. The fuselage fell on the station*

24 Merchant shipping being attacked in the Channel during the first phase of the Battle of Britain. Much of the conflict took place over the sea at this stage

these incidents are not represented in the ground and this is important to bear in mind when considering the impact of 'aviation archaeology' on the record. The events of 29 August resulted in Hillary's Spitfire, L1021, being recovered but scrapped. Pinckney's Spitfire, R6753, was excavated in 1976, and again more recently, remaining the only manifestation of the occasion in modern times (**colour plate 10**). The whereabouts of parts pulled out in 1976 are unknown, while some of the more recently recovered parts have been dispersed on the open market. In other cases the machines have either not been located or are unrecoverable. By end of the Battle so the losses over Britain gradually moved back more across the sea and over the continent.

Phases of the Battle

The RAF squadrons of 11 Group (south-east England) (**61**), dispersed amongst a number of airfields such as Hornchurch, Manston, and Hawkinge, were called into play by Fighter Command whose increasingly-efficient use of radar made it possible to avoid expensive and wasteful patrols. Aircraft, principally Hurricanes and Spitfires (in a ratio of about 2:1), were summoned and directed as needed. The most effective tactic the Luftwaffe could use was to send in waves of bombers to attack targets that made defence essential. The Messerschmitt Bf 109 pilots, already hampered by range, were now obliged to defend the bombers. If they peeled off to confront approaching Spitfires, the Hurricanes could move in and pick off the bombers. High bomber losses could not be sustained and, in any event, they were going to be needed to support an invasion.

In reality this comparatively simple scenario, which on the face of it seems to guarantee a British victory, was confounded by a host of entirely unpredictable factors. Firstly, radar was in its infancy and tracking incoming enemy aircraft required a great deal of practice and guesswork. Secondly, the experience of the pilots varied enormously. Many of the Germans, for example Adolf Galland and Wernher Mölders, had cut their teeth over Spain during the Civil War. Some of the British had learned hard and fast over Dunkirk, for example the surviving members of No. 92 Squadron.

There are many ways of interpreting the progress of the Battle of Britain. Even if the main events will not always have been evident to the men at the time, it is necessary to find some sort of chronological structure. Although certain episodes or phases are now distinguishable, it would be wrong to presuppose that they reflect deliberate intent on the part of either side. Much of what happened seems to have been a reaction to events. These phases have been alluded to above in the discussion of how the record was formed and its effects. In summary they are:

Part 1: 10 July to c. 7-10 August
To begin with the Luftwaffe moved to attack British convoys in the seas around southern and eastern England. Most of the losses, on either side, occurred over the sea.

Part 2: c. 10 August to 7 September
By the middle of August the progression of assaults had moved into south-east England with raids on radar installations, and also airfields. The events of 18 August were particularly important in this transition. The underlying strategy was to break Britain down in preparation for an invasion in late September. This meant destroying British aircraft of all types, but with an emphasis on fighters and their support installations such as airfields, and also any ground units of the RAF.

The effect was to move German and British losses to over the English mainland which allowed the easier recovery of fit British pilots and their return to combat, as well as the recovery of repairable fighters. For the Luftwaffe the results were severely elevated losses of men and machines which could not be made good with replacements. British losses, on a daily basis, were equally dire but stocks of reserve machines and gradually-improving manufacturing capacity meant that the losses could be accommodated longer than Germany could.

Part 3: 7 September to c. 30 September
This phase saw a fundamental change. German assaults were transferred to London and were more directly aimed at the civilian population. This was an interesting alteration of policy. Until now there had been an element of chivalrous restriction of conflict with Britain to armed forces (obviously not executed in Poland or in France). It had reflected Hitler's inherent respect for, and fascination with, British culture (one his favourite films was *The Lives of a Bengal Lancer* — he was impressed by how a small but highly-trained army could control a sub-continent). The failure of the British to surrender frustrated him, as had raids on Berlin by the RAF. The paradox that, had Britain capitulated she would have proved to be unworthy of the esteem in which Hitler held her, does not seem

to have occurred to him. Within this phase, plans to invade Britain were shelved. There was a marked reduction in losses of British aircraft.

Part 4: c. 30 September to 31 October

This is perhaps the most false phase of the Battle because the nature of the air war now settled into a pattern which would last some time beyond. During this month and thereafter the bombing attacks were biased to the night and essentially became the Blitz. Hough and Richards (op. cit., xiv) attribute the inclusion of this phase 'primarily to define the limits within which aircrew would qualify for the Battle of Britain clasp'. The truth is that German losses diminished extremely fast once the bombing was moved to the night, because ground defences were almost completely ineffective in darkness and Fighter Command lacked suitable aircraft or skills to engage the bombers decisively in the air.

These neat divisions obscure the fact that plenty of circumstances on a daily basis conspired to make individual days within phases completely different from one another. On 10 September 1940, just one British aircraft was lost due to enemy action. The following day, 41 British aircraft were damaged or lost. This was partly due to the Luftwaffe preparations for the 11th when two major formations of German bombers were sent over England accompanied by a substantial fighter escort. Other factors, such as the weather or the numbers of experienced pilots (as opposed to novices) available, helped dictate daily events and figures. In this respect every day was its own 'Battle of Britain', and for some individuals one or two days were all that they would experience.

Aftermath

The Battle of Britain was conducted mainly by day, even though scattered night raids took place. It was characterized by intense and brief bouts of aerial combat which led to large numbers of aircraft, British and German, crashing into the ground, mostly in south-east England (**25**). The Battle was followed by the Blitz (see Chapter 6), in which the Luftwaffe continued to conduct bombing raids over Britain but predominantly at night to avoid the catastrophic and unsustainable losses incurred by day. This reflected the Luftwaffe's failure to win control of the sky, but also led to Fighter Command's development of dedicated night-fighter aircraft fitted with radar and suitably-trained pilots which ultimately even denied them control of the night. For the meantime though the chances of a Luftwaffe bomber crew being shot down were hugely reduced and there are consequently far fewer crash sites pro rata for the post-Battle period.

For the day-fighter pilots the battle was moving over the sea and the continent. The tone was now offensive, rather than defensive. In 1941 Fighter Command often operated with Bomber Command in massed attacks; the latter's aircraft were supposed to draw out the Luftwaffe fighters, which they did but with the consequence of significant RAF losses, despite the benefit that more than half the Luftwaffe's strength was eventually moved to the Eastern front. In the context of this book, it means that most of the battles and crashes took place beyond Britain and thus have little or no manifestation in the archaeological

25 The remains of Dornier Do 17Z-2 of 9/KG 76 near Leaves Green (Kent) after the battle of 18 August 1940. Damaged by anti-aircraft fire from Kenley during the raid it was finished off by Hurricanes of No. 111 Squadron. A panel bearing the swastika survives today in the RAF Museum at Hendon

record. There was no hard-and-fast rule about this. In early 1941 No. 66 Squadron incurred two fatalities on 11 February over France but the following day more of its pilots were bounced over home territory. Four Spitfires were lost and two pilots killed while on patrol over south-east England in an incident effectively indistinguishable from those typical of Battle of Britain. However, the RAF had begun to take the initiative but it would be a long time before it achieved air supremacy over German-held territory. Here, notwithstanding the night bombing of Britain and the development of the German unmanned V1 and V2 weapons, it would remain.

Today, there is little trace of the momentous months in late 1940. Only the excavation of the machines which had remained where they crashed has brought some of the frozen moments of the air war back into the frame. Whether these digs were, or are, worth the effort, and how they help us understand a period of history so well recorded in other ways, remains to be seen.

3 The aircraft

Having now looked at the historical background to the Battle of Britain it will have become fairly obvious that, for a relatively short time, a large number of aircraft were involved in intensive aerial battles. These took place normally by day and mostly over south-east England. It was not unusual in the late summer and autumn of 1940 for several dozen aircraft to crash daily in Kent, Sussex and Essex, and others far beyond in the south-west and across the Midlands. It was these crashes and the graves of victims which, apart from the airfields, now represent the principal archaeological manifestations of the Battle. The Blitz had different consequences and we shall look at those later.

A fighter aircraft of the early 1940s weighed between 2,500 and 3,000kg and was manufactured from a variety of metals, wood, fabrics and plastics. A German bomber might weigh well over 10,000kg. Although physically substantial, much of the volume of each machine was void, though within were a number of more massive units, principally the engines and armaments, themselves consisting of guns, ammunition and bombs. Aircraft also contained volatile liquid fuels and of course the bodies of the crew and their personal equipment and effects. They all resemble one another in these respects and this means that the physical remains are broadly similar, with the exact state always being dictated by the precise nature of the crash.

British aircraft design

Many of the participating aircraft are still household names. The Supermarine Spitfire played a lesser role in the Battle than the more numerous Hawker Hurricane whose more basic structure and design made it cheaper to produce and repair. In the longer term the Hurricane was superseded and only the Spitfire remained in production, albeit in a long series of upgraded forms, throughout the war. In spite of the modifications, which eventually led to a long-nosed version with a more powerful engine (the Rolls-Royce Griffon) and variants in wing design, it is the classic form of the Spitfire I (an airframe essentially common to the Mark II which also took part in the Battle, and the Mark V which did not) that remains the aircraft's most familiar image.

In their absolute basics the two machines resemble one another. This is scarcely surprising. Military aircraft development was partly stimulated by the issue of Air Ministry Specifications. The Ministry decided what it wanted in terms of performance, armament, and ease of production often shared amongst various specifications for completely different machines. The requirements were listed and issued to manufacturers who would then compete to win an eventual order; even so, the requirements were liable to change before any new aircraft had been designed. The result was an ongoing process of thinking, development, pre-empting, and innovation which depended on luck as well as judgement. Along the way many problems had to be resolved.

In the end the Hurricane and Spitfire emerged as monoplanes, powered by the Rolls-Royce Merlin engine (**26**), using similar controls, carrying a single crew member and were armed with eight .303 calibre Browning machine guns. Beyond that they differed enormously. The Hawker Hurricane is often described as having grown out of a 'tradition' of earlier wood and fabric biplanes. Looking back more than sixty years later, 'tradition' seems a curious word to use to describe a technique and design which was barely more than a generation old in the mid-1930s. It is important to remember that many of the aircraft used in the Second World War were designed, or at least conceived, in the 1930s. Many people working in the industry had been born Victorians and some had learned their trades before the mass production of the internal combustion engine. It is truly remarkable how much had been learned in the space of a very few years, and it is scarcely surprising that the aircraft industry incorporated some techniques which belonged to an entirely different age.

Nevertheless, it is a truism that technological development almost invariably involves increased complexity both in design and the process of manufacture. Machines, tools, or processes at an early stage of their inception are generally produced by one person, or at least no more than a handful of people. This is true, regardless of whether one is dealing with Iron Age weapons manufacture or early beam engines of the Industrial Revolution. In aviation it was routine for early aviators to build their own aircraft, though they usually depended on buying in engines. This self-reliance is an essential part of the initial process of transferring a concept to a tangible form.

Power and drag

Despite the development of design, the basic process of aircraft manufacture did not alter a great deal during the Great War and in the 1920s. Lightness was a prerequisite of all aircraft design, not only because the force required to lift an aircraft into the air should always be minimized and thus spare power for forward motion, but also because engines of the early twentieth century were not very powerful. Inefficiency in engine design and the low octane rating of the fuel meant that low weight was absolutely essential. However, metallurgy was still at a relatively early stage of development. Many of the light-weight alloys which we take for granted today were either non-existent or extremely expensive in the first half of the twentieth century. Consequently, early aircraft were built of fabric laid over a wire-braced wooden frame. Integrity of design could mean that this was highly effective and reliable so long as the aircraft was moving in the 'right' direction. Equally, it took very little to turn such a machine into matchwood.

The problem was compounded by drag. Drag is created by the friction caused as the aircraft moves through the air. The greater the surface area which hits the air, and the higher the speed, the greater is the friction and thus the drag. Overcoming drag means a more powerful engine and diminishing the area hitting the air by streamlining the fuselage and wings. Early engines were often 'radial' in design; that is, unlike a modern car engine, the pistons radiate outwards from the central crankshaft on which the propeller was mounted. The appearance is like a seven- or nine-pointed starfish. Mechanically simple,

26 The Rolls-Royce Merlin III engine. The design is 12-cylinders, in a V-configuration of two banks of 6, liquid-cooled motor weighing 1375lbs (624kg), capable of producing 1030 horsepower. Comparisons are difficult, but the power generated is around ten times that of the average two-litre motorcar or today's light training aeroplanes. By the end of the war the Merlin had been so improved that its power had been almost doubled. The engine is also equipped with a supercharger, a sealed fan-and-vane device which makes good the reduction in air pressure with altitude by forcing air through narrow cavities at ultra-high speed. (Courtesy of Rolls-Royce Heritage Trust)

the design relies on air-cooling which saves weight but at the expense of presenting this large and non-aerodynamic 'face' to the slipstream. Liquid-cooled engines were becoming preferred in the 1930s, because their power ratings had improved. Configured in a manner resembling the modern car engine, the pistons stood in line running backward. Being liquid-cooled, the engine could be placed within the fuselage and encased in aerodynamic covers, making higher speeds easier to achieve. Better temperature control meant that lower tolerances in manufacture could be accepted because the components were subjected to less extremes of expansion and contraction, and a more reliable output of power could be achieved. These new engines, and the Rolls-Royce Merlin was the most successful of all, were powerful enough to accommodate their own extra weight from the cooling system and also to serve in all-metal aircraft (**26**).

Nonetheless, the radial engine still had a use and it played an important role throughout the war. The glycol used to cool the liquid-cooled engines was expensive and its plumbing was susceptible to leaks and damage. Many fighters were lost simply because a bullet had created a leak which led to vapour ruining the pilot's view, and the engine over-heating and seizing. Conversely, a radial engine could suffer extraordinary damage, including even the shattering of a cylinder by enemy bullets, and yet continue to run well enough to get an aircraft home.

It was also still believed in the early 1930s that having two wings, one above the other, was necessary for strength and lift and to maximize the rate of climb. The greater wing area provided more opportunity for lift, which is itself produced by having an area of low air pressure above the wing, while the higher pressure beneath the wing pushes the aircraft up. To some extent this was a good idea, given the relatively poor engine performance of the era, but the origin of the belief was an event in 1912 when two monoplanes had broken up in the air. This had led to monoplanes being banned for the Royal Flying Corps (the service arm which preceded the RAF) and meant that as late as 1935 the Air Ministry was still prepared to order the biplane Gloster Gladiator as a fighter. However, two wings created more drag and the complex strutting and bracing for the upper wing made manufacture more difficult.

In other words, aircraft design has been a perpetual balancing act between good and bad properties, prejudice and habit, with the outcome being dictated by the power of the engines and the materials available, the intended purpose of the machine, as well as sophistication and finesse in design and the nature of the competition.

Before looking at the individual aircraft it is important to stress how fortuitous it was that Britain ended up with the means to confront Luftwaffe bombers in 1940 at all. In Chapter 6 the background to the philosophy of bombing is looked at in much greater detail. The underlying trend in the 1930s was a firm belief that a successful air force was an offensive force, using bombing as the spearhead of its power in order to pre-empt the enemy's actions. Thus air defence against the bomber was generally neglected until the mid-1930s, in the belief that resources and technical advances should be devoted to designing and building the finest bombers. The upshot was that the development of the frontline fighters, while initiated by Air Ministry requirements, owed far more to the imagination and inspiration of a small number of men working in private firms than it did to the foresight of the RAF and the Air Ministry.

The Hawker Hurricane

By 1930, only 27 years since the first powered flight, new engines and techniques were becoming available which would dictate the progress and nature of the air war of 1939-45. At the beginning of 1930 the RAF placed into service the brand-new Hawker Hart bomber. A biplane, with two-man crew, it looks at first glance like something belonging to the Great War. However, a number of features marked it out as a major improvement. Not only that, but its physical form placed it firmly in a typological series which led to the Hawker Hurricane. One of the variations was the Hector, which was still in service with the RAF in 1940 (**27**).

Using a variety of Rolls-Royce and Napier engines, these Hawker biplanes of the

27 *Hawker Hector, one of several broadly similar military biplane models produced by Hawkers for service in the late 1920s and 1930s. This type was equipped with a Napier Dagger engine. Nonetheless, its basic fuselage similarity to the Hurricane is obvious. Despite surviving in use until World War II it had been withdrawn by 1941 along with most of its Hawker stablemates*

28 *Hurricane I, P3522, of No. 32 Squadron prepares to take off in a publicity shot of July 1940 at Hawkinge. This aircraft was damaged in battle on 15 August 1940*

1930s were capable of speeds of over 180mph. But having two wings meant more drag, compounded in any case by the fixed undercarriage. Nevertheless, Hawker produced a variety of broadly similar-looking aircraft, amongst them the Fury fighter. With an improved Rolls-Royce Kestrel engine and its streamlined fuselage made of a braced steel and alloy girder frame, covered with metal skinning at the front and fabric at the rear, it could reach the then almost unimaginable speed of 223mph.

The Hawker Hurricane was deliberately based on the Fury (**28**). As a monoplane it was a radical departure in British military aircraft design, despite the developments being exhibited by the monoplane racing seaplanes competing for the Schneider Trophy. The inception of the Hurricane is an interesting example of the marriage of two essentially separate tracks in design. As the Hurricane was being designed under the auspices of Sidney Camm, Hawker's chief designer, so Rolls-Royce was developing an inline, water-cooled, V-12 engine which eventually became the 1030hp Merlin. Nonetheless, the outcome was still the product of a relatively small number of people. When it emerged in 1935, the Hurricane illustrated a remarkable combination of progression in thought and design combined with some of the simpler design techniques of what was already an earlier era. In the long-term the latter would stand the Hurricane in good stead when it came to manufacturing in large numbers and easing operational repairs, but would also guarantee it an early demise from service compared to aircraft which were more wholly modern.

This is a phenomenon still evident in the world today. In India, a variety of machines, noticeably versions of the British Morris Oxford car and the Royal Enfield 350cc motorcycle, have remained in production throughout the twentieth century because their lack of sophistication makes them easy to manufacture, and (more importantly) to service and repair 'in the field'. By the same token, and looking further back, it is comparatively easy for enthusiasts to produce flying replicas of aircraft of the Great War or to maintain examples of 1930s aircraft. The Douglas C-47 'Dakota' twin-engined military transport, also manufactured as a civil airliner, is one such example, many of which still earn a living for their owners despite being around sixty years old. This even includes examples with a combat history. In contrast, obsolete aircraft of the 1950s are extremely difficult to restore to a legally-acceptable flying condition because of complex electronic and other systems.

In February 1938 one of the new Hurricanes managed a record average speed of 409mph in a flight from Turnhouse (near Edinburgh) to Northolt (Middlesex). Compared to the Hart this was a breathtaking achievement, in spite of the tail wind, and it emphasized the modern aspects of this new machine. As a monoplane with enclosed cockpit and retractable undercarriage, it appears to be a comprehensive departure from 'tradition'. In reality it was not as modern as it appears. A detailed glance reveals that the principal difference is the lack of the upper wing and associated struts. The profile of the Hurricane and its basic structural design belonged firmly to the Hawker biplane stable, reflected in its internal structure (**29**). This is not in any sense to diminish the timeliness of its completion, and the foresight of Hawkers which had planned to produce the machine in very large numbers long before the Air Ministry woke up to the prospect of war and the alarming rate of aircraft development in Germany.

29 A section of airframe wreckage from Hurricane I, P2680, of No. 607 Squadron (Tangmere). Crashed at Stilstead Farm, East Peckham (Kent) on 9 September 1940, flown by Sgt. R.A. Spyer. The heavy-gauge steel tubes formed the frame, which was stressed by bracing wires, each end of which was threaded for tightening to the correct tension

Other improvements, mainly the three-bladed variable-pitch propeller, made the most of the Hurricane design. It had serious advantages over other, more advanced aircraft. Not only could minor damage be repaired more quickly, but its undercarriage opened outwards to give a wide wheel-base which meant it was stable on grass fields and, as it turned out, on aircraft carriers. During the period of the Battle of Britain, Hurricanes always constituted the largest ratio of fighters. The elevation in proportion of Hurricanes from 38 percent at the beginning of July 1940 to 47 percent by mid-September (Bowyer 1991, 13) is attributable mainly to the decline in use of the Bristol Blenheim, and a slight drop in the proportion of Spitfires. This reflects the ease of manufacture and repair which the Hurricane enjoyed, traded against inferior performance compared to the Spitfire I.

The requirements of the moment and the events of 1940 immortalized the Hurricane in the history of aviation but this to some extent disguises the empirical nature of the design process. It was not a particularly scientific sequence of events and relied almost as much on chance and good luck as anything else, as Hawkers' later experiences illustrate. The appearance of the Merlin engine on the scene was a vital ingredient, and it was the use of the advanced Merlin XX engine in the Hurricane II which kept the aircraft competitive.

Meanwhile Hawkers, once again led by Camm, were already developing the Hawker

Typhoon, and then the Tempest, as replacements. Although these machines, which came into service later in the war, played a valuable and vital part in a low-level attack, strafing and bombing role this was not what they had been designed for. Conceived as a fighter, the Typhoon was plagued by design problems, mainly with the engine. What was beginning to emerge was that British liquid-cooled piston-engined design had really reached its reliable limits with the Merlin and Griffon engines. The Rolls-Royce Vulture engine was a happy disaster because its demise for this project and the Avro Manchester bomber led to the creation of the Merlin-powered Lancaster. The Napier Sabre, eventually used in the Typhoon and Tempest, was severely handicapped by reliability problems. This was not particularly surprising given that it had 24 cylinders arranged in two horizontal banks of 12, making servicing alone a nightmare. Starting failure on the ground was, for example, followed by the laborious process of removing and cleaning all 48 spark plugs (all such aero engine have dual ignition systems as a safety feature, and thus two spark plugs per cylinder). That the average car has only four such plugs, makes the point. Worse still, the Typhoon experienced structural failures including, remarkably, a fault that caused the tail to fall off. Finally, its performance when working properly was so poor at high altitudes that it might have been abandoned had it not turned out to be first-class in a low-altitude role so long as the engine kept running.

The rest of the story of the Typhoon and Tempest belongs outside this book. The point here is to illustrate the seemingly almost random process in developing and designing aircraft. It explains the odd mix of old and new techniques and the reliance on tried and tested procedures wherever possible. For every eagle there were many turkeys, most of which few have now even heard of. It is no coincidence that today, no Typhoons or Tempests fly and extremely few survive at all. Had the effort that was poured into those machines been expended on jet aircraft, perhaps the history of the air war might have been very different.

The Supermarine Spitfire

Broadly speaking, the Spitfire grew out of the same requirements that generated the Hurricane and consequently there is a certain amount of resemblance, in part dictated by the use of the same power plant. Supermarine had, however, been intimately involved with the Schneider seaplane competition, its S.6B model winning not only the Trophy but also the World Absolute Speed Record of 1931. Chief Designer Reginald Mitchell was perhaps less hampered by retrospective habit and more stimulated by the aerodynamic developments created to win those seaplane trophies, and innovations which were taking place in Germany.

Moreover, unlike Hawkers, Supermarine had not spent the late 1920s and '30s producing a successful series of military biplanes and was perhaps therefore freer to experiment. In fact, one of Supermarine's designers, Beverley Shenstone, later recorded that he was originally interviewed for a job by Camm at Hawker in 1931 and firmly instructed that any future single-seat fighter would be a biplane (in Price 1977, 31), a view Camm was shortly to abandon. In this respect it is easy to see why the Spitfire bears no obvious resemblance to any stablemate predecessor, whereas the Hurricane is typologically very similar to earlier Hawker products.

30 Spitfire V, BM597. This machine, built in 1942 at Castle Bromwich, has been restored in recent years and now flies at air displays. During the war it saw service with No. 315 Squadron from May 1942 to February 1943

Nonetheless, the process of development was little more scientific than at Hawkers. The wind-tunnel, for example, was scarcely used because it was not good enough to reproduce real conditions and thus real and valid results. And, like the Hurricane, the Spitfire was initially hampered by being fitted with a fixed-pitch twin-bladed propeller which hopelessly failed to exploit the potential of engine and airframe, thus diminishing the whole.

The distinctive thin elliptical wing form was adopted because it was already known to have advantages when it came to manoeuvrability, and also for minimizing drag, but the design was difficult and time-consuming to manufacture. Similarly, the speed and performance partly relied on the surface rivets being flush with the skin, which added to the labour-intensive disadvantage of the design. Both these techniques had already been experimented with elsewhere, for example on the German Heinkel 70 transport (though its internal wing structure was quite different). As well as the theoretical advantages, the psychological impact of the Spitfire's image on the people who designed and built it should not be overlooked. The fact is that the Spitfire was regarded as instantly appealing and as an icon. It has retained these qualities unchallenged. However much this may have to do with the role it played in the Second World War, it is as likely that it is purely attributable to the form being pleasing. Were it otherwise, there are plenty of aircraft which might have usurped its symbolic role. There is no doubt that the Spitfire's visual appearance was as important a part of sustaining and motivating its design and production

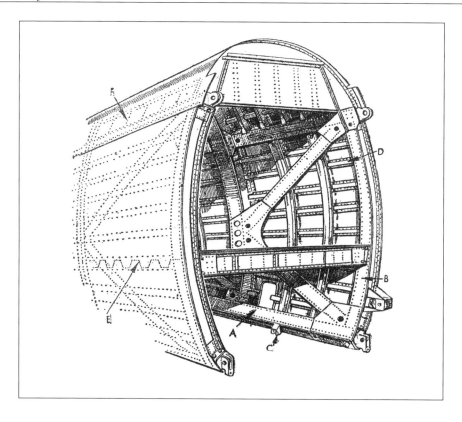

*31 Monocoque-type construction, in this case for a Whitley bomber. See also **32, 42***

as its characteristics. This explains its perpetual popularity and the existence of a small army of manufacturers whose lives are dedicated to keeping Spitfires in the air (**30**, and **colour plate 30**).

But the Spitfire's differences from the Hurricane went beyond superficial appearance. No wood was used in its airframe and no fabric apart from the elevator covering. The design was of the monocoque type, which means that the inherent strength is sustained by the stressed surface, in this case made of sheet steel (**31**). There is some resemblance to the modern car in this respect. Old cars used to be built on a chassis, a heavy frame in which the engine and transmission were installed and over which the body was lowered. Modern cars consist of a box forming the body, into which all the other components are fitted. The strength is reliant on the integrity of the box. Of course, an aircraft is subject to many more stresses and strains than a car and so reinforcement is required in the form of internal frame members (the 'formers') which help dictate the shape, allow heavy loads to be distributed throughout the structure and provide supports for control wires, electrical and hydraulic systems.

The monocoque structure of an aircraft is much more difficult to build than a braced-girder frame. The latter can be tightened and pulled as necessary with wire braces during manufacture. The skin, having no structural role to play, is applied rather than built up and can be easily repaired. In the Spitfire's case, the oval-shaped formers had to be strung out on a jig, and then secured to one another with 'longerons' (horizontal girders), which held each former vertically in the correct spacing (**32**). This created the internal structure that dictated the Spitfire's external shape. Sheets of skinning were cut and bent to the correct shape, and were strengthened themselves with Z-shaped stiffeners.

Absolute accuracy was essential throughout the process, unlike the manufacture of the Hurricane, which was more tolerant of gradual adjustment to correctness. Finally, the stressed-steel skinning sheets were individually riveted into position. Damaged or poorly fitted sections would obviously seriously disrupt the structure's integrity, and thus ongoing operational repairs to machines damaged in combat were more time-consuming.

For anyone unfamiliar with aircraft design it may be difficult to appreciate the implications of very small errors in manufacture. This is in fact quite normal to the extent that no two aircraft will ever be exactly the same. The present author has flown four nominally identical Cessna C152s of similar vintage, yet each offers slightly different performance and handling, characteristics that are consistent to the extent that they contribute to an individual machine's personality. In normal conditions the parameters of the controls and the modifying effect of the trimmer makes good any problems. A trimmer, correctly set, allows an aircraft to fly in a predetermined attitude almost 'hands-off'. No trimmer, or a poorly-set one, means continual application of force to the controls. However, a defect, while virtually undetectable to the naked eye, sometimes has more serious effects. One Spitfire II (P7525) was reported to have a poor diving speed and an uncorrectable lean to the left. On minute examination it was found that the body of the tailplane sat slightly proud where it met the rudder, thus deflecting air away from the rudder and preventing the latter from exerting its maximum influence on the Spitfire's behaviour. The error amounted to no more than 3 or 4mm. With this corrected and a few alterations made to other control surfaces, the Spitfire was declared to be normal.

This case highlights the problems inherent in the manufacture of the Spitfire. The numbers of modifications and corrections introduced throughout its career runs into hundreds and we need not worry about them here. In practical terms the Spitfire absorbed around twice as many man-hours as a Hurricane during its manufacture for an improvement in performance that looks marginal on paper but which, in combat with the advanced Messerschmitt Bf 109E, could be the difference between life and death.

Boulton-Paul Defiant and others
The other aircraft used in the Battle of Britain played such a small role that there is no need to examine their design in much detail. However, the much less well-known Boulton-Paul Defiant is interesting to the extent that it had a two-man crew armed with only a rear-facing gun turret. Once more, shape and form owed more to initiative and chance than anything else. The turret was a French design, hawked around aircraft manufacturers in 1934, and the concept happened to appeal to Boulton-Paul. The idea was sold to the Air Ministry, which produced a specification and invited bids, on the basis that the end-product would act as a stable gun-platform stationed ahead and below oncoming bombers. That the putative foe might not be prepared to co-operate seems not to have been considered.

32 A Spitfire assembly worker. The vertical fuselage 'formers' are in place, awaiting the horizontal 'longerons' to connect them

33 The ill-fated Boulton-Paul Defiants of No. 264 Squadron. PS-V is L7026, lost on 28 August 1940. Behind it is PS-A, N1535, lost on 24 August. While approaching a Defiant from behind was potentially suicidal, approaching from the front was almost harmless as the Germans discovered

When a prototype aircraft was produced by Boulton-Paul, the result was another example in the basic typological series of single-engined monoplane fighter. All metal, and using the Rolls-Royce Merlin, the new machine was recognized to be a high-quality product and it was eventually commissioned in preference to Hawker's pitch for the same specification, the Hotspur. Unfortunately, the initial performance tests were made on a machine that had not been fitted with the turret. Ironically, the figures suggested that had the Defiant been equipped with the same guns as the Spitfire and Hurricane it would have been at least as good. Once the turret was installed, and the Defiant entered production, the most obvious defect was the reduction in top speed to under 300mph, quite apart from the complex manufacturing process which meant that output was very slow.

At the beginning of the Battle of Britain, just 3 percent of Fighter Command's machines were Defiants. In combat their losses were out of proportion to their numbers once the Luftwaffe pilots appreciated the Defiant's shortcomings (**33**). Paradoxically, the basic appearance was initially misleading (they looked like Spitfires or Hurricanes, and an attack from behind looked promising). But the Defiant was swiftly rumbled and Bf 109 pilots simply attacked them from the front or underneath. Hideous losses on 19 July and 24 August led to the type's withdrawal as a day-fighter and its conversion for use as a night fighter (see Chapter 5). Finally the type ended its days as a gunnery practice target tug, where the defects were less relevant.

Other aircraft used in this role included the Bristol Blenheim If, a twin-engined fighter (bomber versions were also used) which was outclassed by 1940 due to its poor armament, lack of speed and poor rate of climb. Any improvement in armament meant more weight and simply diminished the performance further. Experiments with its use as a night-fighter showed some promise but the arrival of the Bristol Beaufighter, a superior twin-engined fighter-bomber which was only just becoming available, ended its prospects (**76**).

The numbers of these aircraft involved were small, constituting altogether 26 percent of Fighter Command's establishment by the middle of September 1940. In time, the Defiant and Blenheim were phased out completely. British bombers, principally the Vickers Wellington (**19**) at this stage but including also the Handley-Page Hampden and the Armstrong Whitworth Whitley, were not integral to this part of the air war though it must be stressed that they were playing an important role in developing the tactics and strategy of Bomber Command and contributing to attacks on Luftwaffe bases in France. It perhaps reflects most of these different types' lack of overall importance in the Battle and the greater scheme of the war that none flies today, bar a single Blenheim, while one flyable Beaufighter approaches completion at the time of writing.

German aircraft design

German use of bombers as a fundamental component of the campaign against Britain meant that more models were involved in any day during the Battle of Britain. These were principally the Heinkel He 111 (**1**, **34**), the Junkers Ju 87 ('Stuka') (**10**, **16**), Ju 88 (**38**), and the Dornier Do 17 (**22**, **25**, **73**) and Do 215. These differed vastly in performance and detail but, apart from the out-classed Stuka which was rapidly phased out in the west, they were twin-engined. Two classes of fighter were involved. The Messerschmitt Bf 109E performed better in some respects than both Spitfires and Hurricanes, whilst the twin-engined Messerschmitt Bf 110 was inferior in all respects apart from range and firepower. The well-known Focke-Wulf Fw 190 radial-engined fighter was a later development and played no part in the period with which we are concerned.

Whereas British single-engined fighter design and production had produced three different aircraft suitable (or thought to be) for frontline combat, the Germans had concentrated their efforts on one single-engined model. By 1945 around 33,000 examples of the Messerschmitt 109, in all its variants, had been produced, more than any other aircraft. It too was the result of a competition to fulfil criteria laid down by the government and its adoption in the mid-thirties came at the same time as the British government was accepting the designs of the Spitfire and Hurricane.

Although to students of military aviation and others interested in the mechanics of modern warfare the differences between the Messerschmitt and the British fighters have always been of immense interest, the fact is that in a typological sense they were very similar. Developments in aviation were remarkably international, caused to a large extent by the movement of aircraft around the world, the colossal expense of development, and also the posturing of the countries involved. This, together with the fact that many models represented different solutions to the same problems, made it almost inevitable that the similarities would be numerous.

The Bf 109 was thus powered by a liquid-cooled V-12 engine, in this case inverted or 'upside down', using types made by Jumo (Junkers) and Daimler-Benz (**35**). It is perhaps even more remarkable to learn that the prototype example was powered by a Rolls-Royce engine (in this case a 695hp Kestrel, an engine which was being used in many of the

34 *The Heinkel He 111 production line. Originally masquerading as a civil airliner design this machine became the standard Luftwaffe bomber of the Battle of Britain period. During the war and after, the type was also built by Casa in Spain, a small number of which are extant and in flying condition*

35 A restored Daimler-Benz inverted V-12 engine, a type fitted to the Messerschmitt Bf 109 and 110. The small oval openings in a row at the bottom are the exhaust ports. The ammonite-shaped assembly at the right is the supercharger, a device which used a fan to compress the air and fuel mixture, thus increasing pressure and compensating for the loss in air density with altitude. The propeller was attached to the shaft at the far left

Hawker biplanes), and that to this day many of the flyable 109s, built under licence as Spanish Hispanos, are powered by Merlin engines. Even the prototype Junkers Ju 87 (Stuka) dive bomber was first flown with a Kestrel.

In terms of structural complexity the Bf 109 was not dissimilar to the Spitfire, having a monocoque airframe with riveted plates for the skin (**36**). A major difference was that the 109 was used in the Spanish Civil War, which meant that by the summer of 1940 the aircraft had been through several model variants, each developed in the light of experience. Thus the Bf 109E, which flew in the Battle of Britain, superseded the B, C, and D models and enjoyed the advantage of a fuel-injection engine which prevented temporary fuel starvation in a dive which afflicted carburettor engines (such as the Merlin). The Spitfire and Hurricane were, however, still flying in their Mark I configurations, albeit with minor modifications and improvements introduced along the way (many in the light of experience during the Battle of France).

It is interesting that the basic similarities, together with the various advantages and disadvantages of other features, combined to produce two first-rate fighters which were so evenly matched. The Spitfire I had better manoeuvrability and visibility and a slightly higher speed. The 109E was better armed (it had three cannon and two machine guns) and

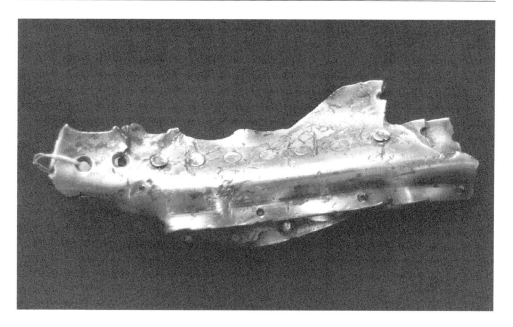

36 Section of airframe skinning from Messerschmitt Bf 109E (Wk no. 4816) which crashed at Gate Inn, near Elham (Kent) on 29 October 1940. Note the flush rivet heads for maximum aerodynamic efficiency, a very labour-intensive part of the manufacturing process. Length 205mm

could fly higher, but oddly lacked an adjustable rudder trimmer which made flying more arduous and exhausting. In practice, the individual skills of pilots, combined with precise circumstances, meant that these differences were marginal. The Hurricane, however, despite its better turning circle, was significantly slower. Nevertheless, in the hands of an accomplished pilot such as Sgt James ('Ginger') Lacey, who shot down at least 13 during the Battle along with several other 'probables' or damaged, the Hurricane could be a deadly foe for an inexperienced German in a Bf 109. However, pilots of the latter reserved more normally their respect for the Spitfire (**37**).

It is remarkable, on the face of it, that Germany, despite her technological advances and quality of manufacture, continued to rely throughout the war very much on variants of models produced by 1940. This was also in spite of the strenuous and successful efforts made to disperse and improve production in increasingly dire circumstances. Only the Focke-Wulf Fw 190 made a radical impact later in the war, and even that involved a reversion to an air-cooled radial engine, seen at the time as distinctly less sophisticated. The introduction of a jet fighter was late and in too few numbers to be decisive. The Allies had the benefit of the arrival of American fighters in the form of the Thunderbolt (P-47), Lightning (P-38) and Mustang (P-51), as well as the higher mark Spitfires and the Typhoons and Tempests. Likewise, the Germans never really developed four-engined bombers, partly thanks to their loss of air superiority so early in the war, and the result was dependence on core models like the Junkers Ju 88, and the Ju 87 (Stuka). Even when the latter was hopelessly out-classed in the west it was extensively used in the east.

37 Messerschmitt Bf 109E-1 (Wk no. 6296) of Stab III/JG26 in a field at Northgate, near Margate (Kent), where its pilot, Oblt Bartels, force-landed after a dogfight with an unknown Spitfire on 24 July 1940 and was imprisoned. RAF personnel are examining the machine's equipment

Part of the reason for this odd state of affairs lay in recent history. During the war itself from 1941 onwards the Allies enjoyed increasing air superiority, and were able to draw on North American resources. Together this made it possible not only for new models to be conceived and tested, but also built in very large numbers. Although unused in Europe, perhaps the ultimate product of this was the Boeing B-29 Superfortress which, with its pressurized crew compartments, computerized gun turrets and exceptional high altitude performance, wrought a terrible revenge on Japan. Like other Allied aircraft built just before the war, such as the B-17 Flying Fortress, it had been designed more or less exclusively for the theatre in which it was used. German aircraft, however, had generally been designed and built earlier, and under conditions in which it was essential to hide the scale of the nation's rearmament.

Rearmament was, in any case, technically illegal under the Treaty of Versailles, drawn up at the end of the Great War. Consequently, machines like the twin-engined Heinkel He 111 bomber, already in production by 1936, were designed from the very beginning with a parallel innocuous civil role in mind. This had the advantage of allowing problems to be ironed out and modifications introduced, but meant that Germany's armaments industry was slightly hamstrung by depending on increasingly obsolete models. The Dornier Do 17 dated back as far as 1932. As the bomber war moved into Germany so the possibilities of designing, testing and producing new machines became extremely difficult, not only because of the practical obstacles but also thanks to political infighting and power

38 The Junkers Ju 88, one of the most versatile of all of Germany's aircraft, and used as a day-fighter, night-fighter and bomber

struggles. The result was that competent new designs like the Heinkel He 219 twin-engined night fighter were produced in hundreds (in this case less than 300) rather than the thousands of its direct competitor, the de Havilland Mosquito. The Junkers Ju 88 was the most modern of the German bombers and had never been intended to act as a civil transport (**38**). It was therefore a more effective competitor when it came to aerial combat. Despite its shortcomings in terms of armament and armour it remained in production throughout the war in an almost limitless range of applications.

Mass production

The differing names and manufacturers conceal the fact that many components were shared amongst these machines, whether British or German. The Rolls-Royce Merlin III engine (**26**) powered almost all the British front-line fighters (a few Merlin II engines were still in service) and the individual power plants were quite likely to have a service life in more than one aircraft. One example had a remarkable career. Merlin III, no. 19281, was manufactured by Rolls-Royce in Derby in February 1940. It was sent to the

Supermarine factory in Southampton and installed in Spitfire I, P9492, itself allocated to No. 74 Squadron, on 29 March 1940. On 25 August it was removed, presumably for overhaul (the Spitfire was transferred to No. 222 Squadron in September and was destroyed on the 30th). The engine was subsequently fitted to Hurricane I, V6846, on 10 November 1940. The Hurricane concerned served with Nos. 3 and 17 Squadrons before the engine was removed on 22 April 1941.

By now the Merlin III was becoming obsolete as the new Merlin 45 became available for the Spitfire Vs, and the Merlin XX for Hurricane IIs. Nonetheless, after a year of idleness, engine no. 19281 was installed into an old Hurricane I, P3829, then with No. 760 Squadron, on 2 May 1942. About two months of service followed but it was taken out again on 4 July before being fitted to a Defiant I, M1682, used as a target tug by No. 10 Air Gunnery School. A flying accident led to its removal, for the final time, on 28 June 1943. It survives to this day, intact, on display in Derby Industrial Museum where it is on loan from Rolls-Royce.

Plainly therefore, an excavated engine from a Battle of Britain site may have had a significant history which has no connection with the airframe in which it was found. Unfortunately, it is unusual to be able to trace an engine's career. The records concerned were largely destroyed at the end of the war, and it is only thanks to the survival of private notes that some information subsists.

The same applied to the German forces, the Junkers Jumo 211 motor being used in several different machines for example the Ju 87, and Ju 88, and some models of the Heinkel He 111. Versions of the Daimler-Benz used in the Bf 109 were also used in the Heinkel He 111. Of course this was a logical consequence of mass-production and the same principle applies in the modern car industry where different models conceal the fact that many use the same powerplant. Even during the war itself these engines underwent improvement and development rather than outright replacement. It is worth reiterating the point made in the previous chapter that German engines exhibit markedly greater levels of engineering finesse than British ones. Whether this made them better or worse is not the point; what matters is that they absorbed more effort and expense in their manufacture. It simply takes more time and money to assemble engines with roller-bearing crankshafts, and better rocker bearings (**plate 22**).

The archaeological record of Battle of Britain aircraft

The survivors

Some of the participating aircraft survived the Battle of Britain, and indeed even the war itself. The latter applies almost exclusively to British aircraft, though a small number of German machines are involved. In Britain's case this was usually because the models had become obsolete and had been withdrawn from front-line service. By mid-1941 the Spitfire Marks I and II had been outclassed by the Spitfire V which would itself be replaced by a variety of versions but principally the Marks IX, XIV and XVI (intermediate marks were either experimental, limited in production or used for specialized roles). Improvements to the Messerschmitt 109 and, later, the advent of the Focke-Wulf Fw 190

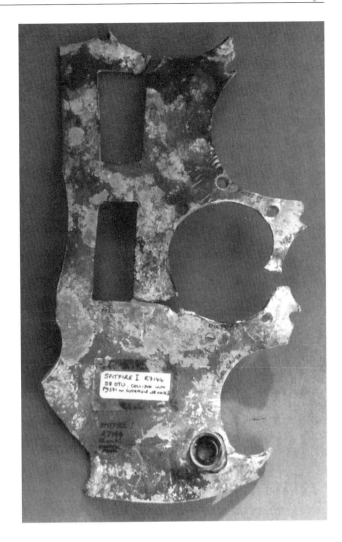

39 Right-hand section of the instrument panel from Spitfire I, R7144. As is usual the thin steel and delicate construction of the actual instruments means they have not survived, apart from as unrecoverable fragments of glass and rust

in northern Europe made developments essential. Consequently, the Spitfire I's combat history is almost entirely confined to the period of the Battle of Britain and before, reflected in its distribution in the ground today as wreckage. It was manufactured on into 1941 but few saw service outside training units. Indeed, the sole surviving Spitfire I in flying condition today, AR213, has just such a past. The Spitfire II remained useful in combat for longer, some even remaining in this capacity until 1944.

But in the circumstances of war it was unlikely that many 1940 machines would still be functional in 1945. Spitfire I, R7144, was a relatively late Mark I which first flew in February 1941 (**39**). Although it spent much of 1941 with No. 132 Squadron its obsolete performance and specification condemned it to a life largely with training units where it met its end in a collision on 18 December 1943.

Many others were scrapped when hostilities ended. The pattern is repeated throughout human history. The various phases of Hadrian's Wall, built by the Roman army in the 120s

AD, are viewed as historical and archaeological enigmas by those who study the Wall and its features. As a military project it was entirely routine to pour resources into the frontier when it was needed and to abandon it when it was not. Normal considerations of cost simply do not apply during war. Within days of the war in Europe ending in 1945 German civilians were employed by the Allied command to cut up and burn perfectly good US fighters then based on German airfields. In south-east Asia large quantities of brand new American aircraft spare parts survive from the Vietnam War, still in their packing cases where they were abandoned (Woodley 1999).

Machinery, however, is not easily reusable should circumstances require it, unless the materials can be recycled. Hence the scrapping of redundant aircraft. Nevertheless, it is regrettable when this results in there being no extant examples. The potency of the Spitfire has ensured otherwise. But contemporary bombers such as the Short Stirling now survive only as crashed relics. The Handley-Page Halifax presently on display at the RAF Museum in Hendon is the only original Halifax to survive in Britain and it had to be recovered from the bottom of Lake Hoklingen in Norway where it was lost after a raid on the German battleship *Tirpitz* in 1942 (**colour plate 8**). The bizarre fates that might befall aircraft components is no better illustrated than the recent identification of Halifax bomb doors serving as garden cloches in Elgin (Grampian), now recovered for use in a restoration of a Halifax at Trenton, Ontario, in Canada.

However few Spitfires and Hurricanes, or Luftwaffe aircraft, of the Battle of Britain survived in 1945 only a handful survive today. A small number were allocated to museums during or shortly after the war. The most authentic in appearance is Spitfire I, X4590, which resides today in the RAF Museum at Hendon. It saw service during the Battle, with Nos. 609 and 66 Squadrons, but was withdrawn from frontline service early in 1941 from where it went to a series of training units before being allocated for museum display. An earlier Spitfire I, P9306, reached the RAF in late January 1940. By July it was with No. 74 Squadron at Hornchurch and participated in the Battle from here and at various other bases to which the squadron was moved. It was withdrawn from frontline duty in September and thereafter was transferred to a variety of units. In August 1944 it was selected for museum use and was shipped to Chicago's Museum of Science and Industry where it remains to this day.

Spitfire I, R6915, is now displayed in the Imperial War Museum in London (**40**). This aircraft was active throughout almost the entire period of the Battle with No. 609 Squadron. Like the Chicago machine a variety of subsequent movements and withdrawal from combat service followed. In 1946 it was installed in the Imperial War Museum and it has continued to hang from the ceiling ever since, fortunately untouched by a well-meaning restorer and it thus retains an authentic patina though its blue and red fuselage roundels are post-1940. Hurricane I, L1592, now in London's Science Museum, was with No. 615 Squadron during the Battle, incurring heavy damage when it crash-landed at Croydon on 18 August 1940. It was repaired and also embarked on a varied life in RAF Maintenance Units. In 1963 it was restored to its Battle configuration before display.

None of these machines is, then, truly original. Some have been displayed in markings belonging to their later lives. All have experienced damage of some sort and wartime repairs. Indeed it was their luck to be damaged in ways which were not terminal, leading

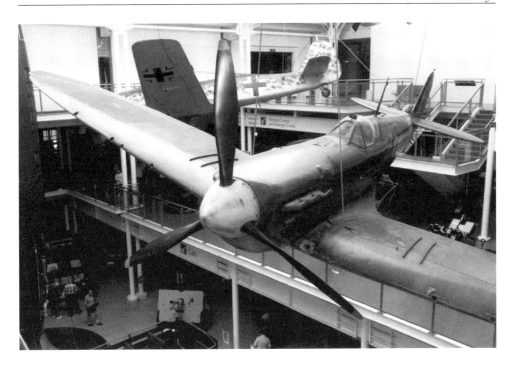

40 *Spitfire I, R6915, as it survives in London today. The machine saw action in the Battle of Britain with No. 609 Squadron*

to their withdrawal from frontline service. But the repairs and movements prevented them surviving in their precisely original form. A single fighter which saw service in the Battle, the celebrated Spitfire II, P7350, remains airworthy with the RAF Battle of Britain Memorial Flight but this has inevitably been at a price. The original engine has long since been replaced and other parts of the airframe have been repaired and modified though the aircraft remains, rightly, the most treasured of all Britain's surviving Second World War aircraft. Quite apart from its nature as a military aircraft, it belongs to that select band of obsolete products of human industry and imagination which remain serviceable.

Just one flyable Messerschmitt Bf 109E (Wk no. 3579) survives at the time of writing, and a very few others of later marks. Its restoration was completed in 1999 and it resides in the Museum of Flying in Santa Monica (California). Eventually such machines may outlive all their human contemporaries, but flying these aircraft is a dangerous business and reflects the vast number of accidents, let alone battle casualties, in wartime. A Bf 109G, the so-called 'Black 6' crashed at Duxford in 1997, bringing to an end several years of flying displays which had followed a long period of restoration (**178**). In September 1999 one of the Spanish-built 109s, used as make-do substitutes for German Bf 109s at air shows, crashed in Sabadell, Spain, killing the expert display pilot, Mark Hanna.

The loss in recent years in Britain of the only flyable Mosquito, and a Lockheed P-38 Lightning, both also fatal accidents, have raised the question of whether it is in the long-term historical interest to keep these machines in the air at all. The Bristol 'Blenheim' on the current airshow circuit (in fact a Canadian-built version called a Bolingbroke) crashed after restoration a number of years ago, and a second, protracted, restoration had to follow. But these aircraft were built for flying and there is no doubt that they are most easily understood and appreciated in the medium for which they were built. Certainly those who fly them have no doubts. It is also worth noting that at least one aviation archaeologist has used his excavation experience to good purpose, and now runs a business called Airframe Assemblies which manufactures airframe components from new which are used to keep Second World War aircraft in flying condition, and as a consequence helps maintain skills which might otherwise be lost. The Spitfire V, BM597, which features on the front cover of this book and elsewhere, is only flyable today thanks to new parts made by this firm and several others. In the long run though it is probably inevitable that flying examples will be complete replicas.

These individual aircraft therefore do not survive in the archaeological record (as it is normally understood) but their existence is of primary value. Unlike conventional archaeology we possess artefacts in their approximate original form. This makes it possible for us to reconstruct and understand crashed aircraft. Wrecked and broken artefacts are only coherent if we know what they looked like prior to destruction. It needs only passing familiarity with a single crashed fighter of 1940 to see that someone faced with the remains in the twenty-fifth century, and who lacked any basis for reconstruction, would be presented with an almost insurmountable challenge. There is an analogy with conventional archaeology. The archaeologist attempting to reconstruct an Iron Age wooden structure from a handful of postholes has no model on which to base his ideas. He or she can only guess, using common sense and imagination. The outcome cannot be tested and this will inevitably affect the accuracy of the interpretation of circumstances. Where we know what the original looked like, this is not the case.

Recovery and repair

In Britain the convention was to attend to a crashed aircraft and, so long as they were not buried deeply, remove or conceal the remains where they were German. British aircraft were removed also but repaired where possible. On 20 October 1940, a Messerschmitt Bf 109E-4 (Wk no. 2780) broke up in the air when it was shot down over Welling (Kent) by P/O Bryan Draper in a Spitfire II of No. 74 Squadron. Therefore, instead of driving itself into the ground with maximum force, the wreckage fell in large fragments onto the surface. Once the usual triumphant photographs had been taken (**41**) the remains were carted off to be scrapped, never to be seen again. The pilot, Oberfw. A. Friedemann, baled out but his parachute failed to open and he was killed. Draper's Spitfire (P7355) was also damaged and he force-landed. This machine was repaired and remained in service until 1944.

Intact German aeroplanes were removed to RAF bases for examination and in some cases restoration and test-flying. A Messerschmitt Bf 109E-3 (Wk no. 4101) which saw service in the Battle of Britain survives today at the RAF Museum in Hendon thanks to a force-landing at Manston on 27 November 1940 (**colour plate 9**). Others were placed in touring exhibitions used to raise funds and in some notable cases were even shipped to North America for the same reason, suffering a variety of fates. A Bf 109E-4 (Wk no.

41 *The wreckage of Messerschmitt Bf109E-4 (Wk no. 2780) of 6/JG52 in Wickham Street,
Welling, in south-east London after crashing on 20 October 1940. This aircraft broke up in
combat with a Spitfire of No. 74 Squadron, causing dispersal of the wreckage in mid-air, and
thus diminishing its impact. In this view the underbelly of the aircraft is visible with the propeller
blade visible just left of centre. The wheels of the main undercarriage can be seen on either side*

1190), which force-landed after engine failure at East Dean (West Sussex) on 30 September 1940, and spent the rest of the war in the United States and Canada, ending up in Ottawa in 1945. Not surprisingly, little was done to conserve it and the machine ended up rusting away in storage in Ontario before being purchased from a scrap dealer in the early 1960s and brought back to Britain to face another 30 years in store. The aircraft, or rather what remains of it, has now been acquired by the Imperial War Museum at Duxford where it is being restored into a condition that will reflect its force-landing and also its experiences in North America. But a large number of components have had to be sourced from elsewhere or built from scratch. Others have also survived in British and American museums but the majority of German aircraft were left in the ground where they had fallen, or scrapped during the war and their metals used in the manufacture of British aircraft. In a curious variation from this practice the metals of some were used to manufacture small alloy bells with a cast inscription recording their source, and were sold to raise money, for example for the RAF Benevolent Fund.

But rather more remarkable than the re-use of melted down aircraft has been the discovery of large buried caches of Luftwaffe aircraft components at Freeman Field, Seymour, Indiana. Used originally as a training base, by the end of the war in Europe it had become a storage centre for aircraft from America and, more interestingly, from elsewhere. Luftwaffe machines were shipped over in 1945 on the British carrier, HMS *Reaper*, for evaluation. But with hostilities at an end, the importance of trying out obsolete aircraft at a time when the technology was racing ahead became rapidly of little concern. While the better-preserved machines were retained for display the authorities were left with enormous quantities of aircraft, components, service items and airfield paraphernalia. What was not sold, given away or melted down, was buried in large pits on the site in the late 1940s. Documentary records of this activity led to searches in the early 1990s which have now begun to yield large quantities of engine parts, propeller blades, and parts of airframe. Obviously there is an interesting archaeological aspect to material being located so far from its origin, even though the historical background and surviving records provide a straightforward explanation. But it is also true that the burial grounds are likely to yield parts and other equipment, no examples of which are otherwise extant (Thole 1999).

The fate of British aircraft which fell into German hands is less easy to discover. On 23 May 1940 Spitfire I, P9373, crashed in France and was left where it fell. Excavation in 1999 revealed that none of the crucial parts, such as the reflector gunsight, had been removed though evidently the wings had been cleared away at some point. On the same day Spitfire I, K9867, of No. 74 Squadron, force-landed in France and was captured intact by the Germans. The RAF record card merely reports that it 'failed to return'. The evidence for its fate relies wholly on the extant German photographic record (Price 1990). What happened to the machine itself is entirely unknown. Similar records of another Spitfire, N3277, of No. 234 Squadron, show that after a force-landing in France on 15 August 1940 it was painted with Luftwaffe markings and eventually fitted with a Daimler-Benz engine. Thereafter it disappears from history though this particular Spitfire has earned itself a curious immortality. The scale-model kits manufactured under the label 'Airfix' have, for many years, included a 1:72 version which carries the markings of this aircraft.

Where British aircraft crashed in Britain were concerned, the first priority was to decide if the machine was repairable. If so, the wreckage was removed to one of the repair depots, such as No. 1 Civilian Repair Unit at Cowley (Oxon). Here usable components were salvaged or the airframe was mended and put back into flying order.

These repairs introduced an interesting complication. When an aircraft was first 'taken on charge' by the RAF it had a serial number (allocated during manufacture) which at this date consisted of a letter followed by four digits (later, two letters followed by three numbers). The serial was lightly stencilled in pencil on either side of the rear fuselage and then painted in by hand. It was also stencilled on some internal components, sometimes during the repair process to keep associated parts together. The latter are usually identifiable in crash wreckage when they turn up but it is very unusual for the external fuselage number to survive. Various other numbers and marks appear throughout the aeroplane. Airframe parts prefixed '300' denote Supermarine components for the Spitfire I (**42**). The engine had its own serial number, as well as quality-control stamps consisting of RR in a small circle. Some components, like compasses, gunsights, and oxygen connectors, bear AM below a small crown for the 'Air Ministry'.

The aircraft serial was recorded on Air Ministry Form 78 (**43**) which was also supposed to carry the serial number of the engine, though this was rarely included. The units to which the machine belonged were then entered by hand and these notes record the various movements from squadron to squadron. In practice many machines changed hands only once or twice before being lost. Typically the Form 78, known often as the 'movement card', records the RAF Maintenance Unit who initially received the aircraft, then the squadron, perhaps No. 603 'City of Edinburgh', before adding the date of its loss in combat.

Where a machine was extensively repaired it was possible for more than one Spitfire to be turned into a single example. Though the serial number of one might be retained there is an interesting parallel with the modern illegal practice of welding together two halves of different cars but retaining the registration mark of one, or perhaps even a third car. Two Spitfire IIs (P7309 and P7365) of No. 603 Squadron were lost close to one another near Brede in East Sussex on 25 October 1940. One machine has now been substantially excavated but without confirming its identity. Although the engine number survived on several components its omission from the aircraft's movement card renders it useless as a confirmation. The excavated machine is almost certainly P7309 but this cannot now be verified.

Problems of course exist with the records. The Hurricane I, P2617, presently displayed at the RAF Museum at Hendon is now known to have participated at least briefly in the Battle of Britain (Saunders 2000). This is in spite of its own records stating that it was undergoing repair for minor damage throughout the period and not being returned to combat duties until November 1940. The confirmation that it saw service during the Battle has only come to light in the logbook of F/Lt J.M. Bazin who flew it with No. 607 Squadron out of Tangmere on 11 September 1940. This example illustrates the incompleteness and fallibility of official records which is scarcely surprising considering the intensity of effort expended at the time. That a machine was serviceable at the moment needed was of considerably more importance than bothering to check that its presence was recorded.

42 Section of Spitfire airframe former, bearing the serial number 300... denoting a Spitfire I. From the wreckage of L1067 XT-D of No. 603 Squadron, flown by S/Ldr G.L. Denholm on 30 August 1940. Crashed at Snargate (Kent)

This confusing situation affects the Rolls-Royce Merlin III engine in other ways. As we saw earlier, its interchangeability meant that individual examples might serve in several different aircraft. But this was rare, and it is even rarer to be able to show this. The case outlined earlier in this chapter is exceptional. The motors lasted up to, at most, about 240 hours in service life before a major overhaul. Active for perhaps at least three to five hours daily during the Battle, this is equivalent to around 48 consecutive days of operations, rather longer than most machines were liable to survive. Even in service life, extreme conditions and use of emergency boost (additional power) could markedly shorten engine life. The Spitfire I, K9807, of No. 603 Squadron, which arrived at the unit on 29 September 1940, was fitted with an engine (Merlin III no. 24527) which had been despatched from Crewe on 1 September. Having been in action since the Battle of France, apart from a period out for repair between late August and September, this was at least the aircraft's second motor and very probably its third or fourth. It crashed on 5 October, ending its service career which had begun in October 1938 as one of the first Spitfires built.

Merlin III, no. 19035, was manufactured in July 1940. In February 1941 it was lost when a Hawker Hurricane I, Z7010, crashed on a delivery flight. This much is recorded on the Accident Report Form. But Rolls-Royce records state that in December 1940 the engine, which was built later than the aircraft. had been overhauled by Sunbeam. The engine's history is now untraceable but it is very likely that this overhaul followed service in other aircraft and that it had seen combat service in the Battle of Britain. Indeed, it may have been removed from a crash site and repaired whilst the crashed aircraft itself was scrapped.

AIRCRAFT

A.M. Form 78.

Contract No. *527112/36*

Type.. *HURRICANE I* ...... R.A.F. No.. *L2071* ...... Contractor *Hawker's*

Type of Engine ...... *Merlin III* ...... Engine Nos.. *5103 – 119727*

	(1)	(2)	(3)	(4)	(5)	(6)	(7)	(8)	(9)
Taken on Charge of	46 Sqdn	229 Sqdn	253 Sqdn	229 Sqdn	85 Sqdn				
Date taken on Charge	22.8.39	9/5/40	20/5/40	24.5.40	20/7/40				
Authority	1632	1623A	16230	1623DA	1623ØA				

	(10)	(11)	(12)	(13)	(14)	(15)	(16)	(17)	(18)
Taken on Charge of									
Date taken on Charge									
Authority									

Date	Unit to whom allotted	Authority	Date	Unit to whom allotted	Authority
6.8/7/39	46 Sqdn	15772			

43 Air Ministry Form 78. Original forms are mostly damaged and difficult to read. This version has been modelled on an original, and reproduces the movement details for Hurricane I, L2071. This machine was first allocated to No. 46 Squadron, on 22 August 1939. Its timely transfer to No. 229 Squadron on 9 May 1940 shows that it narrowly escaped being sent to Norway with No. 46, most of whose Hurricanes were lost in the sinking of HMS Glorious on 8 June 1940. However, it was lost on 1 September 1940 while on the establishment of No. 85 Squadron. It was piloted by Sgt G. Booth who later died of his injuries

Recoverable and reusable aircraft had normally belly-landed, that is they had landed horizontally, usually with their 'wheels-up'. This resulted in damaged components on the aircraft's underside, a bent propeller and perhaps a wounded pilot. Sometimes, despite superficial or even significant damage, it was possible for a pilot to fly back to his base (or any base) and make some sort of landing there. In either case the aircraft would be repaired or pirated for parts and thus be withdrawn from any potential archaeological record.

More often the pilot had baled out or been killed, leaving the aircraft to career into the ground or sea. Such crashes meant the aircraft was destroyed beyond repair. This takes us back to the physical structure. Being principally a void within, combat aircraft usually quite simply collapsed on impact into unrecognizable heaps of metal skinning and ribs. But the engine was different. The lightness requirement for aviation engines meant a light alloy casing containing unavoidably heavy steel components like a crankshaft, cog wheels and bolts. In facing forwards, they naturally pulled the aircraft down and, depending on the angle of the crash, would enter the ground first. Having fallen from as high as 15,000ft or more these engines were quite capable of being taken by their momentum down to five metres or more below the surface.

Considering that these engines might have been turning over at up to 3,000 revolutions per minute (or 50 times a second) it is not surprising that many self-destructed. This was even more likely to occur where the propeller blades were metal (as most were). The blades struck the ground and forced the engine to stop with the effect that many of the heavier internals threw themselves through the aluminium engine casings. In short, they often blew apart as they powered into the ground at impact speeds of up to 600mph. The RAF Maintenance Units or private contractors attending such incidents rarely had the manpower, time or plant to extract engines in this condition. In marshy soil the possibilities were even more limited, while at the same time allowing the engine to go even deeper.

A Brighton company, A.V. Nicholls and Co., was engaged to help No. 49 Maintenance Unit in 1940, the unit principally responsible for recovery in the south-east. Not only were there many aircraft to deal with but No. 49MU had also lost a lot of their own equipment in raids on airfields. On 25 November 1940 the Nicholls Company's two-man recovery team set out to retrieve the remains of Spitfire II, P7386, which had crashed at Sandwich on 14 November. They made an assiduous effort to pull out the engine which, after two days, they finally located at a depth of just over six metres. Despite working on until the 27th, flooding foiled any attempts to extract it. The job was abandoned and the engine is believed still to be there. Another mark of the chaos involved was the attempted recovery of the wreckage of Spitfire I, R6922, of No. 92 Squadron which crashed at Tuesnoad Farm, Smarden (Kent) on 19 October 1940. Failing light meant the wartime recovery crew used hurricane lamps. One lamp was knocked over and ignited the aviation fuel in the debris. The operation was abandoned and backfilled. Excavation of the site in modern times produced not only the aircraft's remains but also the burnt-out hurricane lamp.

Although outside the main sphere of this book, the activities of the United States Eighth Air Force are interesting in this field, not least because some of the incidents attended by officials are particularly well documented (not common in this subject). On 21 February 1944, two B-17G 'Flying Fortress' bombers of the 385th Bombardment Group collided on their way home from a raid on Diepholz in Germany. Both aircraft were flying at a height of about 1000ft and were destroyed. They fell less than half a mile apart into marshland near Reedham (Norfolk). The B-17 was a large, four-engined, bomber which (in the case of the G model) carried a crew of ten. Contemporary photographs of the USAAF recovery team show that at both sites the machines were scattered across the swampy surface in the form of barely-recognizable heaps of smouldering airframe and other machinery (McLachlan 1989).

One of the B-17s (42-37963) fell sufficiently close to higher land to put it in reach of hawsers and winches secured on the firmer surface. This, at any rate, is the only reasonable explanation for the failure of modern excavation work to locate anything other than a pair of propellers, many small fragments of airframe and a few of engine casing, and the machine guns from the forward turret. In fact, analysis of much that was recovered proved to have belonged to the forward compartments of the fuselage. The conclusion can only be that almost all the aircraft was recovered in 1944 by the USAAF, even to the extent of removing the engines, no trace of which has ever been identified apart from a very small number of tiny fragments.

44 One of the engines from a B-17G Flying Fortress (42-31370) is hauled out of Reedham Marsh in 1999, where it had fallen on 21 February 1944

The other aircraft concerned (42-31370) fell far enough further into the marsh to put it out of easy reach of major recovery equipment. Although the site was undoubtedly visited by the USAAF and much of the wreckage removed, it is plain from subsequent recovery expeditions (McLachlan 1989, 79-95), including one attended by the author in 1999, that much larger parts were abandoned, confirmed in a letter from one of the US recovery team which had been responsible. These included at least three of the engines and propellers, which were generally recovered from significant depths of four metres or more in the marsh (**44**). Part of the depth may be attributed to suction and sinking long after the accident but the fact remains that pressure of time and resources precluded the easy recovery of major pieces of crashed aircraft, despite the concern to remove ugly and demoralizing evidence of fatal crashes. In the end, out of sight was out of mind and as good as out of the ground. In many cases this was where the aircraft, or parts of them, were left. Despite the differing treatment of the wrecks both were recorded as 'salvaged' on official records.

In built-up areas the buried engines were even more likely to be left where they were, because recovery would have involved further surface demolition. For this reason, the Hurricane I, P2725, of No. 504 Squadron, flown by Sgt. Ray Holmes, remains below the surface of Buckingham Palace Road where it fell on 15 September 1940. Holmes baled out and lived to tell the tale. But the RAF Maintenance Units were mainly concerned with recovering human remains wherever possible, or to deal with aircraft which had a future in service.

The consequences were usually that surface wreckage was cleared but that the engine and other heavy pieces were often abandoned. Considering the priorities of the time this is not very surprising and over the succeeding four or five years officialdom forgot about such sites, though they remained recorded in local police reports as well as government papers where they are traceable today. In the years following the war farmers became accustomed to the depressions in their fields, and perhaps the occasional recovery of fragments of airframe from plough-soil. But in general little or no trace of most of these crashes was visible on the surface, remarkable when one considers the drama involved in the high-speed impact of a warplane. The remains beneath the surface, however, generally tell a very different story.

4   Excavating the air war

An understandable reaction to the prospect of excavating aircraft from the Battle of Britain is to say that, as we know what the machines looked like, there is no need. One might equally say that as Neolithic stone axes and Roman pottery are also fairly well known there is no need to bother to recover them either. There are plenty of other artefacts about which the same or similar could be said. If the sole purpose was to recover artefacts then perhaps it would be true; and it might also be said that therefore there is no reason *not* to dig them up either in whatever cavalier fashion takes the excavator's fancy. But an air crash is the same as any other archaeological feature, with the usual exception that it was created in an instant rather than as an accumulation over time (nevertheless, coin and other treasure hoards also represent 'instantaneous' deposits).

The existence of documented history of the air war means that many individual stories can be told without excavating the physical remains of aircraft involved. Indeed, little or none of the history could ever actually be extracted from the ground through excavation, something that is instructive when considering the excavation of an artefact or site for which there is no documentary evidence. It is not normally possible to reconstruct the sequence of events that led up to the physical manifestation of an event in the ground. The episodes described in this chapter are representative of the randomness of events at any time, and especially in a war. It is precisely this unpredictability which dictates the procession of events yet which cannot be reconstructed without the kind of data that the archaeologist is normally deprived of.

What then, does excavation add? Perhaps it is worth first considering the alternative point of view. Where there is no prospect of recovering the 'historical' background it is debatable whether excavation is worth the trouble at all. For example, the excavation of a prehistoric stone circle will never tell us anything about the leader (or group) who was able to motivate his or her people to build the circle. Equally, it will never tell us if there was some catastrophic natural event, or war, which provoked a crisis leading to a desire to control the environment through a spiritual medium. It may tell us how, or approximately when, the circle was built. It will never tell us why. Worse, it is impossible to ascribe, with certainty, a function to an artefact unless we have unequivocal contemporary documentary evidence (or its equivalent) which tells us. All else is speculation which, in a vacuum of certainty, is often accorded the substance of facts and treated as such.

But where a prehistoric circle is concerned, there is no choice. Excavation, or at any rate surveying and measurement, is the only means of generating a theory or answer. Sadly, we can never know if we are right. Where aircraft are involved we often already know how it came to be where it was, its history, who was in it and something about the pilot. We can also talk to people who were there. But this all remains only part of the picture and there is also the essential ingredient to excavation — in digging we reach out to the time ourselves and cross to the event in question.

Archaeologists often indulge in the vanity that their work is exclusively for 'scholarly' purposes and deny any existence of a fascination with the passage of time and the powerful desire to witness the past in the most direct and tangible way we can. This is a curious facet of our age, an intense need (apparently) to deny the existence of any straightforward, almost childlike, unconditional curiosity. In the past, antiquarians had no problem with this and it is to the credit of aviation enthusiasts that they have inherited something of the passionate excitement that their professional archaeological peers seem often to have lost, or at least entertain the vanity that they are above such feelings.

It also turns out that excavating aircraft does yield valuable information. Not only that, it may come as a surprise to learn that some of the materials used in the manufacture of 1940s aircraft are highly unstable and decaying at an alarming rate. The Battle of France and the Battle of Britain are not as precisely documented as one might think. The standard of recording varied as the war progressed. Certain theatres of the air war, for example in the Middle East and North Africa, are much less well documented for the simple reason that the units were operating in arduous conditions, often with semi-obsolete equipment and making-do. We have already seen that a trotted-out procession of historical events does not automatically bear up to close scrutiny. The details of individual crashes are also not straightforward and doubt surrounds many of them.

The different materials used in manufacture results in extremely variable rates of survival. Magnesium was valued for being 'the lightest known commercial metal' but is unfortunately 'very liable to corrosion' (Meacock, *c*.1941), something of an understatement. One excavation of a P-51 Mustang which crashed near its base at Duxford in 1944 found that most of the alloy had 'corroded into the familiar blue oxide' (Evan-Hart 1999). Despite the addition of other metals such as aluminium and zinc to inhibit this defect, 1940s magnesium-alloys began to decompose almost immediately even in service, let alone in the ground. Magnesium alloy was used on Spitfires for the control column handle and wheel hubs, amongst other things including (later in the war) air-frame rivets. Such components almost always survive as no more than unrecognizable piles of powder, if at all (**45**, **colour plate 5**). Magnesium was also used in the manufacture of German aircraft. The rocker box covers and some other parts of Daimler-Benz engines (fitted, for example, to the Bf 109) were made of magnesium and these are invariably missing from excavated motors. Aircraft of the Second World War, maintained today in working order, do so with such components remanufactured in modern materials.

The very popularity of the Battle of Britain, elevated by the 1968 motion picture of the same name, has also accounted for the exploration of almost all the accessible crash sites of the period by amateur groups, called variously 'aviation archaeologists' and 'wreckologists'. This is an interesting situation. The groups concerned, provoked by immense personal enthusiasm as well as a collecting instinct and, in a few cases, the prospects of financial gain, have frequently displayed their finds in private museums which are open to the public. The museums at Sandown, Shoreham, Brenzett, Manston (**46**), Tangmere, and Hawkinge which commemorate the Battle of Britain all fall into this

1 The 'Scientific height finder', one of many devices aimed at the wartime aviation enthusiast

2 Group Captain Allan Wright DFC AFC of No. 92 Squadron in 1999 with the gunsight from his Spitfire I, X4069, which he flew on 27 September 1940. A cannon shell from a Messerschmitt Bf 109 entered the cockpit, missed Wright's head, and ricocheted off the canopy before destroying the gunsight. See also **plate 3**

3 (left) Allan Wright's gunsight in close-up. The circular reflector plate has been shattered. In flight the pilot had to rotate the two dials at the bottom while aiming at a target

4 (below) German graves at Hawkinge. Hermann Weber (left) crewed a Stuka of 10/LG1 which crashed into high-tension cables near Folkestone on 15 August 1940. Gerhard Wollin (centre) was killed in a Messerschmitt Bf 110C of 6/ZG26 by Hurricanes of No. 56 Squadron over Folkestone. Helmut Gericke was the only one to die out of the crew of a Heinkel He 111H-3 of 2/KG1, which crashed at Snargate near Dymchurch following assaults by Nos. 65 and 32 Squadrons. The others were captured unhurt but Gericke died from his wounds

5 The firing button from Spitfire I, P9373, shot down on 23 May 1940 in France. The magnesium spade-handle grip has rotted away completely, leaving only the brass button fitting

6 Wing-Commander Peter Olver DFC handles the generator from Spitfire II, P7309, from which he baled out on 25 October 1940. He went to have a successful combat career in Britain and North Africa until he was shot down over Sicily and captured in 1943

7   *Spitfire V, BM597, at Calais in 1999. This is an original wartime aircraft (built 1942) which has been restored to flying condition. Allan Wright, in a Spitfire cockpit for the first time in more than fifty years, discusses the controls with its present-day pilot, Charlie Brown*

8   *Halifax II, W1048, in the condition it was found at the bottom of Lake Hoklingen in Norway. It made a force-landing on the frozen lake surface on 27 April 1942 during an attack on the German battleship* Tirpitz. *It is the only original Halifax extant. Note how the weight of the port inner engine has caused it to snap free from the wing mount. This characteristic explains how engines often separated from the airframe due to the much greater forces of a crash from altitude*

9 *Messerschmitt Bf 109E-3 (Wk no. 4101) of 2/JG51 at Hendon. On 27 November 1940 this machine force-landed at Manston (Kent). See also* **20**

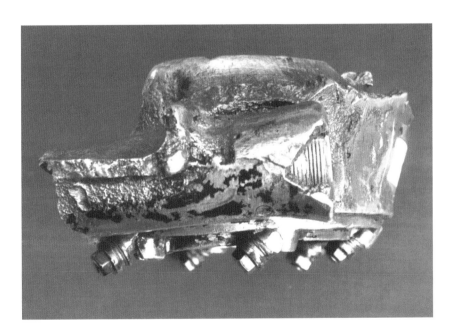

10 *Oil-filter mount from Merlin III engine sump fitted to Spitfire I, R6753, flown by P/O D.J.C. Pinckney. Pinckney flew with No. 603 Squadron and was a personal friend of Richard Hillary who found the former dangling from his parachute in a tree after both had been shot down on 29 August 1940 (*The Last Enemy, *133-4). The bolts have been swept back by the force of the crash which then tore this component from the engine body. Diameter 135mm*

11 *The remains of Hurricane I, P3175, DT-S. Delivered to No. 257 Squadron (Debden) on 9 August 1940, it crashed on 31 August 1940, killing P/O G.H. Maffett. The remains were excavated from coastal marshes at Walton-on-the-Naze (Essex). This is the only excavated example of a Battle of Britain aircraft displayed in a national collection. The wooden propeller blades have snapped off, allowing the engine to slow down without self-destructing. See also* **47, 48**

12 *The gravestone of Sgt. Paul Klipsch at Wierre-Effroy, near Boulogne. Klipsch died on 23May 1940 at the controls of Spitfire I, P9373, of No. 92 (East India) Squadron in the final days of the Fall of France*

13 *The foot pedals from Spitfire I, P9373, bearing the Supermarine logo. Later in the war this refinement was abandoned in favour of a more purely functional design Fragments of the fabric second-position pedal survive. These allowed the pilot to operate the aircraft in a more hunched position during combat, which helped resist blacking-out forces in tight turns*

14 *B-17G Flying* Fortress Mary Alice *(42-31983) or is it? This is actually 44-83735, which
arrived in Europe too late for war service. It was used by the president of Philippine Airlines
before the French* Institute Géographique Nationale *took it over in 1952. Now at the
Imperial War Museum, Duxford, repainted and restored to combat condition for a war it never
fought. The real* Mary Alice *of the 401st Bombardment Group survived the war but was
scrapped at Kingman, Arizona, in 1945*

15 *Washing the Wright-Cyclone radial engine from B-17G (42-31370) after its extraction from 5
metres of marshland near Reedham (Norfolk)*

16 *Pratt and Witney twin-row radial Wasp engine from P-47D Thunderbolt 42-75101, photographed in 1999 on Mynyndd Copog near Bala in Wales where it fell in 1944*

17 *One of the aircraft used by the author, a Cessna C152, sits on the grass at Chichester-Goodwood
(W. Sussex), once Westhampnett airfield during the Battle of Britain. This is one of very few
wartime airfields of south-eastern England which looks and functions much as it did in the 1940s*

18 Replica gate guardian Spitfire IX or XVI at Biggin Hill, bearing the serial number N3194 of the Spitfire I flown by Roger Bushell, squadron leader of No. 92 Squadron on 23 May 1940

19 Remains of the underground fuel dump at Hawkinge

20 *Lydd Airport. Lydd was not built until the 1950s and now serves light aircraft. However, this type of hangar was used extensively during the Second World War. Derelict examples can still be seen around the country, while others have been adapted for industry or agriculture*

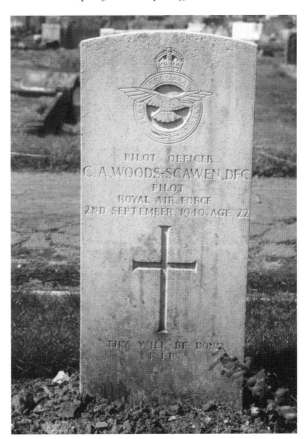

21 *The grave of P/O Charles Woods-Scawen of No. 43 Squadron in the cemetery beside the old airfield at Hawkinge. He died when he baled out too low from his doomed Hurricane on 2 September 1940*

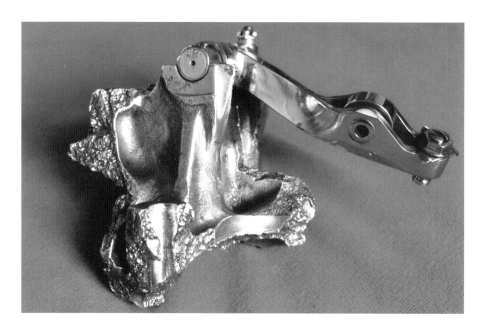

22 *Fragment of Jumo 211 engine from a Junkers Ju 87 (Stuka) which was shot down and destroyed on 18 August 1940 during an attack on the airfield at Thorney Island (Hants). It crashed at Cutmill, West Ashling. The component is an exhaust rocker arm with section of cylinder head. Length of twisted arm 112m*

23 *The propeller of a Spitfire, in this case fitted to a restored Mark V, BM597, and perhaps the most evocative image of the air war*

24 Remains of houses and offices on the west side of Noble Street in the Cripplegate area of the City of London. In the distance is the Barbican development. The destruction here, preserved as a park, exposed the west wall of the Roman fort which housed the London garrison

25 (above) The ruins of Coventry cathedral preserve fragments of the medieval stained glass which survived the fires of 1940

26 An air-raid warden's axe, still clearly marked '1941 ARP'. This axe was used by a Mr A.V. Brayger who served as a fireman during the Blitz in London and Orpington

27 The restored spire of St Augustine Watling Street is all that remains of this church, destroyed in 1940

28 Christ Church, Newgate, London as it stands today, preserved as a ruin and a potent reminder of the conflagration of 1940. Part of the ruined nave was cleared to make way for road development and the church was consequently never restored

29 *A modern museum to London's experiences in the Blitz. By far and away the largest proportion of civilian casualties from aerial bombardment occurred in London*

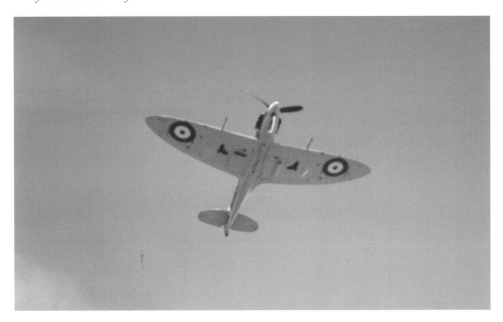

30 *The Spitfires restored to flying condition provide the most enduring symbol, not just of the air war, but all of the Second World War. At the end of the millennium there were more working examples of this legendary machine than at any time since the early 1950s. This example is BM597*

*45 Cockpit and controls of an early Spitfire I. The most prominent feature is the control column with spade grip and firing button. Compare with **colour plate 5** to see what actually normally survives of this feature*

category. Other museums, such as Thorpe Abbotts in Suffolk, commemorate other aspects of the air war, in this case the 100th Bombardment Group of the US Eighth Air Force. This is an admirable outcome but the original priorities were often to extract the engine and controls and leave the rest of the airframe to rot underground. The sheer cost and difficulty of private extraction meant that excavations depended on hard cash provided by the participants and an inevitable partial division of the spoils afterwards by way of recompense. Some of the fragments now circulate on the commercial market and these

*46 Shattered wheelcase (gearbox) from the Merlin III fitted to Hurricane I, P3815, flown by Sgt.
F.J. Kozlowski of No. 501 Squadron on 18 August 1940. The aircraft crashed near Whitstable
(Kent). Kozlowski survived, injured, but was killed in 1943. The visible devices are: generator
drive (far left), magneto drives (top centre), supercharger drive (centre), fuel pump drive (bottom
centre), and starter transmission (far right). The actual starter would fill the void at lower right,
but along with the complete supercharger and carburettor, has broken away entirely. Now
displayed at Manston Museum*

include items from some private museums that were closed along the way.

In some senses commercial disposal is a perfectly practical solution to coping with
large quantities of scrap metal, and additionally helps publicize the history of the Battle
itself. It is also true that a large, rusting, engine (perhaps any engine) means comparatively
little to most members of the public. Displaying dozens of decrepit, rusted and broken
examples in a row, which at least one aviation museum does, is potentially useful to a
specialist but bewildering to the average visitor who is unlikely to be able to distinguish
one component from another. Conventional archaeologists have criticized the large
numbers of these aviation excavations and the unnecessary accumulation of 'similar' finds.
Oddly, this apparently does not apply to conventional archaeologists whose stocks of
pottery and other finds, now stored in museums throughout the country (a very small
proportion is actually displayed), would bury the aviation relics many times over.

The issue of what to do with large numbers of finds has already been explored by more
traditional museums. Within recent decades the practice has been to withdraw large
collections from display, such as pottery, leaving selected items on view. The museum at
the Roman villa at Rockbourne (Hants) is a good example. Originally laid out by the site's

excavator-owner, the museum resembled an antiquarian's den and featured dozens of cases creaking with every conceivable find. Once the site was taken into local authority ownership the museum was transformed into a series of modern displays. This was not entirely satisfactory because it immediately became less useful to a specialist and reduced the museum to the level of a standard 'Roman life' museum, almost indistinguishable from many others in Britain. Of course the main collections are usually claimed to be accessible to a 'specialist' but in practice this means references, paperwork, and dingy store-rooms.

The truth of course is that the 'finds' serve as a medium to the history (**colour plate 6**). The parallel existence of a Roman pot, a Bronze Age dagger, and a Spitfire propeller, at once in their own times and in our own, is essential to the human fascination with the past. We like to see, and handle, these things and imagine what they once were, who made them, and who they belonged to. One of the especially satisfying aspects of the crashed aircraft is that these connections can be made to individuals, sometimes still alive, something which is usually impossible for other artefacts. In other words, they lead us to an individual human experience which can be a priceless experience for those lucky enough to hear a story 'from the horse's mouth' (**colour plates 2, 6**). One wrecked Spitfire is thus not the same as another wrecked Spitfire. It was not unusual for excavations conducted in the 1970s and 1980s to be witnessed by the pilot concerned, fascinated to see a moment of his early career brought up out of the soil and to share his tale with the diggers.

Excavation is not the only means of accessing this record but, as we saw earlier, very little indeed has been deliberately preserved since 1940. Unfortunately, the quasi-commercial exploitation of crashed aircraft has resulted in the kind of random dispersal of components which leads to destruction of this very record. It is of course easy for 'real' archaeologists to criticize this (and they do). But the parallels with the antiquarians of a century ago will be all too obvious. The excavations of crashed aircraft often provoked considerable local, and even national, interest in a period of recent history which was disappearing into oblivion in the 1960s.

But, whatever the shortcomings of amateur aviation groups, it is also true that official bodies have generally attempted to suppress the activities at a cost to general public interest in what was, after all, a seminal moment in modern British history. This is founded in law that protects the Ministry of Defence's property interest in the physical remains of military aircraft. There is also the entirely commonsense consideration that aircraft were armed and the munitions may still present a danger. However, it has been possible for a large number of legitimate excavations to take place and the outcome has sometimes been admirable. Many of the groups pooled and shared their information such that it could be published in the outstanding volume *The Battle of Britain, Then and Now*. This volume is of a quality which compares very well indeed with conventional archaeology syntheses, at least in the sincerity and detail. In this chapter some examples of excavations of American machines from later in the war are included. They help illustrate a broader range of problems, and also the value of revisiting historical events through this route. It may also not be appreciated that a very large number of surviving crash sites in Great Britain belong to the aircraft of the United States Eighth and Ninth Air Forces, especially in East Anglia.

Had it not been for the amateur groups, many of these sites would now be permanently lost under new buildings, new roads, or simply be forgotten as, for example, the youthful farmworkers who saw the crash at the time grow old and die. If these enthusiasts had not pursued their interest when they did then the opportunity to associate digs with living memory and documentary history would simply have been missed.

The Roman treasure found at Thetford (Norfolk) is an uncomfortable reminder of what can happen. The settlement site, of prehistoric and Roman date, was excavated by archaeologists who failed to discover the exceptional Roman treasure. How this potentially disastrous turn of events came to be is another story but is linked with a dogmatic reluctance to use metal detectors even in a controlled fashion. The present author has repeatedly witnessed the inability of trowelling to yield small metal finds, which are then harvested from spoil heaps by detector users working with archaeologists. Happily, most archaeologists are now content to recognize the value of using all available techniques, but at Thetford it took a metal-detector user working illegally, after the site had been passed back to the developers, to find the hoard of gold and silver. Its fundamental importance to our understanding of late Roman Britain is now well-established. The argument expressed in defence of the archaeologists who missed it, that it would otherwise have been left intact for future generations (itself completely unguaranteed), is a nonsensical abrogation of responsibility and a bizarre preference for contemporary ignorance over knowledge and discovery.

Excavating a Hurricane

Whatever the different feelings about digging, extremely few aviation excavations have been conducted with anything approaching the finesse of most professional archaeologists. On the other hand, it is debatable just how appropriate gentle trowelling would be for recovering an aircraft. One of the most outstanding modern recoveries involved the Hurricane I, P3175, which crashed on 31 August 1940, while being flown by Pilot Officer Gerald H. Maffett of No. 257 Squadron, then based at Martlesham Heath. The Hurricane was a casualty of an early morning engagement with Messerschmitt Bf 110s escorting Junkers Ju 88 bombers. Maffett was killed in the fight and his machine crashed into the shingle and sand of the beach near Walton-on-the-Naze (Essex). The aircraft was left where it fell and it gradually sank into the foreshore. In the early 1970s the wreckage was gradually being exposed once more by erosion.

Forays by local enthusiasts revealed that much of the forward area of the Hurricane was still in existence. The rear part of the Hurricane's airframe used a considerable amount of fabric and wood, so it was plain that the identifiable remnants were likely to be all that was left. The use of heavy equipment, careful digging, and delicate separation of components allowed the remains to be lifted. These included the Gloster Aircraft Company's plate which confirmed the machine's identity (**47**). By 1978 the Hurricane had been displayed in the RAF Museum at Hendon in the manner in which it was found (**48, colour plate 11**). The display is extremely evocative and is most unusual in having retained so many peripheral components in their correct configuration. The result is a

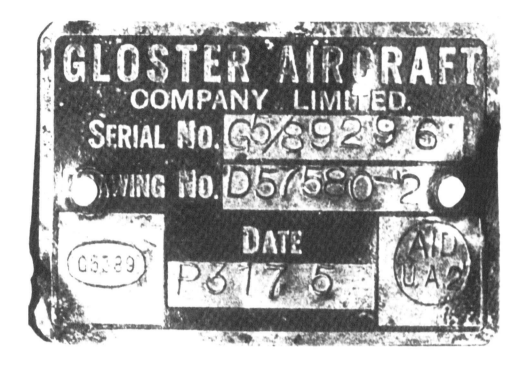

47 *Gloster aircraft plate recording the serial number of Hurricane I, P3175. In 1934 Hawkers acquired the Gloster Aircraft Company, and Hurricane production also took place in Gloster's factory at Hucclecote (Gloucs), producing machines which first flew in 1939. (After the Battle)*

completely coherent forward section of Hurricane, rather than glass display cases of fragmented scrap or freestanding engines on trolleys.

That a pilot died in this machine is an important element in such excavations. Maffett's body was removed at the time of the crash and he was buried at Windsor Road Cemetery, Bray (Berks). This is not always the case and in many instances the deceased pilot was left in the buried wreckage for a variety of reasons. Inaccessibility, oversight, and confusion could all play a part. Nowadays a conflict exists between official organizations and the families of the pilots. There is considerable reluctance to permit the excavation of war graves. It is both illegal, and apparently quite reasonable.

But few families, faced with the prospect of recovering a father, uncle, brother, or grandfather and having him interred in a proper, marked, grave, have any objections to having their relatives removed from their unmarked crash sites. Indeed they may positively solicit it. Consequently, actions brought by the Ministry of Defence against aviation recovery groups have not succeeded, despite being ostensibly favoured by the law as it now stands. Nevertheless, the law is the law, and at present the wreckage of a military aircraft in the United Kingdom, of whatever date or country of origin, is the property of the Ministry of Defence. Permission in the form of a licence from the Ministry is required, as well as that of a landowner, before any excavation can take place. The decision

*48 Hurricane I, P3175, from the rear looking into the cockpit. The control panel survives. The heavy-duty spars for the port wing protrude to the left but the crash has torn off the rest of the wing and the whole starboard wing. Now displayed at the RAF Museum Hendon. See also **47** and **colour plate 11***

has almost always turned on whether human remains are known or thought to exist on the site. Under such circumstances permission is normally denied. Quite apart from the complicating issue that relatives generally prefer to have the remains removed, errors in records sometimes mean that an excavation of an 'empty' aeroplane reveals the crash to be of another machine altogether, and with a body inside.

This is, of course, a crucially different factor from conventional archaeology. Where bodies are recovered from normal excavations the treatment of human remains is normally dignified and respectful, but there is rarely any question of 'bad taste' or desecration involved because the sensibilities of relatives are not a concern. The analysis is normally scientific and considered and the remains are later displayed or re-interred. The recovery of the remains of F/Lt Hugh Beresford, also of No. 257 Squadron, illustrates the issues very well. Beresford was killed in Hurricane I, P3049, on 7 September 1940. His machine crashed at Elmley on the Isle of Sheppey at 5.30pm that evening. His body was never recovered at the time, perhaps due to the relatively remote and marshy crash site, and he was merely recorded as 'missing'. It was not until 1971 that the machine's remains were identified. In 1979 the Hurricane was excavated for the purposes of making a BBC television programme and with the approval of Beresford's sister. The resulting operation located Beresford's remains in the wreckage which were then awarded a full military funeral at Brookwood Cemetery.

There can be no doubt that in this case at least Beresford received the recognition he deserved, and which he would have been deprived of had he been left where he was. But the circumstances of his death provide a graphic example of the work needed to recover some of this wreckage. In conventional archaeology a site will typically consist of an accumulation of features and artefacts which need to be dismantled systematically to identify and record the sequence and nature of deposition. An aircraft represents an assembly of artefacts into a whole, and a single event. It is also buried more deeply than most conventional archaeology. Extraction cannot be satisfactorily or profitably performed with laborious scraping away at the surface. Perhaps the best comparison is the Roman treasure hoard found at Hoxne in the early 1990s. The colossal value of this deposit meant that its notification to the authorities had to be followed immediately by a single day's excavation for the sake of security. This was performed by lifting out the entire feature as a single block and dissecting it in a laboratory. Like a crashed aircraft the treasure hoard represents an assembly of artefacts gathered into a whole and buried as a single event. The deposit is thus a single event, rather than an accumulation of events, at least where such hoards are found in complete isolation from other sites or features of the period (as is normal).

But unlike ancient treasure hoards, crashed aircraft can weigh a great deal. The Merlin III engine's stated dry weight was 1375lb or about 625kg. Although rarely found in a single piece, the dead weight of the central block and its internals is considerable. Lifting this from a depth of five metres in a marsh is no mean feat, and one which requires engineering skills not normally needed on conventional archaeological sites. But, the sheer trauma of a crash can have a devastating and revealing effect on the engine, with the result that the question of lifting the whole assembly does not arise. The following account of the excavation of a Spitfire is an unusually vivid example.

Excavating a Spitfire

This recent excavation of a Spitfire shot down in the Battle of France was accompanied by a great deal of careful research. Although it was not a Battle of Britain casualty, the type of aircraft was exactly the same and the occasion belonged to the same general historical context. What also made the dig exceptional was that it operated as a joint project between aviation archaeologists, well-versed in the practicalities of recovering aircraft, and professional archaeologists working for the popular Channel 4 television programme 'Time Team'. The Spitfire concerned, P9373, of No. 92 'East India' Squadron, was shot down on 23 May 1940, one of the first occasions in which Spitfires confronted German aircraft over enemy territory. That it fell in France is extremely important because it escaped the attention of early recovery teams both during and long after the war, and also escaped the attention of aviation enthusiasts until recently.

P9373's identification in 1998 by the enthusiasts Alan and Anita Brown was timely because the eventual excavation in 1999 was accompanied by a former member of No. 92 Squadron, present on the same sorties in May 1940, as well as the pilot's brother (**49**). This permitted an unusually complete picture to be built up, enriched by the eyewitness

49 Fragment of air-frame bearing the stencilled serial number P9373 which identified the remains of a Spitfire from No. 92 Squadron machine shot down on 23 May 1940 over Wierre-Effroy near Boulogne

accounts of local people in the village of Wierre-Effroy. The recovery was careful and considered and resulted in an imaginative and cooperative venture which not only experimented with the techniques needed to excavate the machine, but also served as a means to revive interest and knowledge in a recent event of our past. Anyone considering the value of indulging in archaeology at all should never underestimate the dynamic importance of directly accessing an event, and not just through the pages of a book.

23 May 1940
Squadron records, and individual log-books, record the events of 23 May in graphic detail. No. 92 Squadron was despatched from Northolt, in west London, to fly sorties out of Hornchurch over north-eastern France in support of the British Expeditionary Force, then being systematically cornered by the German Panzer units, supported by infantry and Luftwaffe dive-bombers. This was a critical moment in the war for Britain. Germany's Blitzkrieg across the Low Countries and into France caused political and social turmoil in Britain as the policy of appeasement, and its protagonists, collapsed. At the end of the twentieth century it is difficult to appreciate the very terrible sense that Britain's existence was under threat, but that was what prevailed and the pilots of No. 92 Squadron were about to find out for themselves that the enemy constituted an unprecedented threat to everything they considered important.

On 23 May the squadron flew two sorties over France in the Boulogne area. On both occasions the pilots flew into trouble. Allan Wright flew on both and recorded his experiences in Blue Section (one half of the squadron), and the squadron's first losses, as follows:

> Morning: Got a long burst at one [Me 109]. Possibly shot it down. Klipsch saw Pat [Learmond] go down in flames
> Evening: Same again, Evening. Met 20 Me 110s, 15 Bombers and 10 Me 109s. Blue Section attacked 110s, shot at about 5, one definite, and followed another over hedges, many pieces flew off. Lost CO, John Gillees, Klipsch, Paddy [Green] at Manston wounded.

The squadron operational report for the day was balder, if more detailed:

> 23 May: The whole squadron left at dawn for Hornchurch where they commenced patrol flying over the French coast. At about 0830 hours they ran into six Messerschmitts and a dog fight ensued. The result was a great victory for 92 Squadron and all six German machines (Me 109s) were brought down with only one loss to us. It is with the greatest regret that we lost Pilot Officer P.A.G. Learmond in this fight. He was seen to come down in flames over Dunkerque.
> In the afternoon the Squadron went out again on Patrol and this time encountered at least forty Messerschmitts flying in close formation. The result of this flight was another seventeen German machines (Me 110s) were brought down and 92 Squadron lost Squadron Leader R.J. Bushell — the commanding officer — Flying Officer J. Gillees and Sgt. P. Klipsch (566457). Flight Lieutenant C.P. Green was wounded in the leg and is now in Hospital at Shorncliffe. The remainder of the Squadron returned to Hornchurch badly 'shot-up' with seven Spitfires unserviceable. It has been a glorious day for the Squadron, with twenty-three German machines brought down, but the loss of the Commanding Officer and the three others has been a very severe blow to us all, and to the Squadron which was created and trained last October by our late Squadron Leader. (AIR 27/743)

The squadron's losses were significant but, at the time, the victories believed to have been gained over the Luftwaffe softened the blow. Nevertheless, the loss of the commanding officer was a psychological disaster so early in the days of combat and, as it turned out, the recorded victories almost certainly were far in excess of the actual numbers gained. Sgt Paul Klipsch was never mentioned again. This was scarcely unusual. In war, the loss of a man is followed by sad reflection and an awareness that it might have been oneself. But, as Samuel Pepys observed wryly of his brother Thomas, who died from illness in his bed, 'But Lord, to see how the world makes nothing of the memory of a man an hour after he is dead' (*Diary*, 18 March 1664). Pilots rapidly learned to cope with the loss of friends and colleagues by putting the events out of their minds.

50 Sgt. Paul Klipsch at the controls of his Spitfire just before he was killed. (Wright)

23 May 1940 had turned out to be a pivotal day for No. 92 Squadron, but Klipsch and the others were replaced and so were their machines. What happened to most of the Spitfires lost that day is unknown. It was not until 1998 that research and field-walking showed that the scattered surface remains of an air crash near the village of Wierre-Effroy belonged to a machine bearing the serial number P9373. This is the serial of a Spitfire I, recorded as belonging to No. 92 Squadron and lost on 23 May 1940. The grave of Paul Klipsch lies less than half-a-mile away in the churchyard at Wierre-Effroy. The association seems immediately obvious though, as the excavation indicated, the story was not completely straightforward.

According to its Air Ministry Form 78 the Spitfire itself arrived at No. 92 Squadron on 6 March 1940. Allan Wright's own log book shows that he flew it on 9, 13, and 18 March, with the initial flight being for the purposes of testing it. Thereafter it seems to have been allocated to the squadron's 'A' Flight (Wright flew with 'B' Flight). Unfortunately the machine belongs to the great mass of Spitfires and other aircraft which were apparently never photographed during their service lives. Even Wright, an exceptionally enthusiastic photographer who took many pictures of the squadron, happens never to have taken an image of P9373 though that which shows Paul Klipsch in the cockpit of a Spitfire may well be this aircraft (**50**). As a result, even the letter code that P9373 wore is unknown. But, as P9372 (photographed in the air by Wright at this time, see **17**) is known to have been GR-G, it is likely that it was GR-H.

Until the excavation, nothing more was known about the precise circumstances of Klipsch's death, apart from the fact that it occurred during the second sortie of the day and involved attacking a significant number of German aircraft. For the pilots, their precise location and the happenings on the ground were unknown to them. For the Martinez family of Wierre-Effroy, the dog-fight in the sky above resulted in a shower of .303

Browning machine gun bullet cases on their home followed by a screaming noise as an aircraft at full throttle came down across their roof and impacted in the field beyond. Villagers who had seen the German army advance through their home made their way to the crash, recovered what they could of the body and buried it. It is not now known whether they knew the identity of the pilot. The present gravestone was erected after the war when the Commonwealth War Graves Commission dealt with military graves in the area (**colour plate 12**). Whether or not German forces in the vicinity took any interest in the crash is obscured by time. Local people describe how some of the Spitfire remained above the ground for the rest of the war. A small number of components, including the aerial, were found in the field ditch where they had presumably been thrown by the farmer.

Although we know the basic story of this Spitfire, its remains can tell us how it came to an end. The wreckage turned out to be a potent and devastating image of war and tragedy. A high-speed, and vertical, impact seems to have resulted in much of the wings being shattered and destroyed on the surface while the fuselage, pulled along by the engine, entered the ground up to a depth of around three metres (**51**). This much can be concluded from the absence of almost all the wing structures, including the undercarriage. These must have been removed at the time, though where to and by whom is unknown. That a great deal of ammunition and some of the guns were left in the soil suggests it was not the German army.

Having struck the ground the engine began to erupt while the fuselage itself followed and collapsed. The outcome was a compacted mass of metal with the engine at the bottom and the tail wheel at the top (**52**). The 9.12m length of the Spitfire had been compressed into a unit little higher than 1.5m, even taking into account the dispersal of debris on the surface, mainly emanating from the wings.

This Spitfire's engine carried its own history. Examination of the components confirmed it as Merlin III, no. 13785, the same engine noted on the aircraft's record card. It had thus retained its original power plant, something which few aircraft later in the Battle of Britain were able to do, that is, if they lasted more than a few weeks. The trauma of impact had several noticeable effects, derived from the consequences for the crankshaft. As the most massive component, and also its high speed of rotation, the crankshaft was severely affected by being slowed down almost instantly. The propeller striking the ground seems to have lost two blades immediately. The retention of one blade will have guaranteed a rapid collapse in engine rotation as it spun into the ground, until the shaft broke out of the reduction gear housing and it separated. We need not consider the details of the mechanics but it is necessary to appreciate that the main rotating element of the engine, the crankshaft, turned a gear on its end at the front of the engine. This gear rotated a much larger gear (the reduction gear) above on which the propeller was mounted.

Unfortunately this was a fundamentally weak part of the engine, even in normal service. The large gear wheel, together with the propeller and its shaft, is a heavy assembly. In normal service its egg-shaped alloy housing at the front of the engine proved inadequate for the stresses and strains involved. Cracks appeared and one Rolls-Royce modification recommended bolting strengthening bars into place. In crashes the large gear, together with the propeller shaft, tended to be ripped out of the gear housing which itself cracked

51 *The entry-hole of Spitfire I, P9373, is clearly visible in the cleaned and scraped surface. The discoloration is caused by disturbance, different moisture content and contamination from aviation fuel and lubricating oil released as the engine exploded*

52 The compacted wreckage of Spitfire I, P9373, showing the tail wheel at the top while the engine is splayed out at the bottom

into dozens of pieces. This was exactly what happened to Klipsch's engine. The entire front part was destroyed and the propeller with shaft and gear exited after initially causing the rest of the engine to slow down abruptly (**53**).

The resistance offered by the crankcases to this abrupt braking was minimal and they also exploded into hundreds of fragments. This allowed the crankshaft to writhe further out of control, compounded by the weak walls of the barrels. Merlin pistons moved up and down within independent steel liners. These were press-fitted into the lower crankcase and protected by a thin wall of alloy, which disguises their true nature. As this weak wall disintegrated the crankshaft was able to wrench the liners out of place.

The consequences were dramatic. Freed from the constraints of a crankcase and bearings the crankshaft, with its flailing pistons now flapping uselessly in their liners, twisted permanently out of true. One of the pistons was, at this instant, at the bottom of its down-stroke. At this point something struck its skirt and split it. The split ends bent outwards and, as the piston was forced upwards on its last up-stroke, they tore into the steel liner and ripped it like a can-opener (**54**). Considering that the alloy used for the pistons is far softer than the steel used for the liner, this indicates the degree of force involved. As the liner collapsed and distorted the piston seized at the top and remained wedged in this position until today, with part of its skirt still protruding from the gouge it had torn. This seizure was too much for the four bolts securing the piston's connecting rod to the crankshaft. Stretched as if they were tubes of soft clay, they narrowed as a tube

53 *The reduction gear and propeller shaft assembly from a Rolls-Royce Merlin III. This example came from a Hurricane (probably P5185, No. 253 Squadron, crashed 1 September 1940) but illustrates the shape and size of a major component, which tended to tear the engine apart during a high-speed crash. The large steel cog wheel alone is 307mm in diameter and 70mm thick*

54 *Piston and rod from Spitfire I, P9373. The piston has seized in its liner and the consequent resistance to the reciprocating force of the crankshaft has caused the connecting-rod joint (left) to tear away from the crankshaft and allowed the complete piston assembly to break out of the engine*

of clay does when it is rolled out, and broke apart. Carried away by the residual upward force which was no longer converted into reciprocating motion, the piston and its liner detached and blew upwards and outwards, along with seven of the twelve others. Constrained by the soil the engine settled more or less in one place but now ruptured into fragments.

This was the history of the bottom part of the engine. The cylinder heads, containing far less substantial moving parts, escaped largely intact but instead of surviving as a parallel pair, one was twisted round and behind the other. This entire process seems to have taken place in a period no longer than half a rotation of the crankshaft. At maximum revolutions a Merlin III was capable of 3,000rpm, or 50 revolutions a second. Merlin III, no. 13785, was transformed from a 1030hp fighter engine into a mass of barely recognizable scrap in around a hundredth of a second. Behind it, the rest of the airframe collapsed like a crumpled paper cone.

The wreckage was in fact fairly typical for a Spitfire (**colour plate 13**) though the engine was in an unusually fragmentary state. Some sheets of skinning from the rear part of the aircraft bear large holes around 25mm in diameter which may have come from 20mm cannon shells. These can only have come from a Messerschmitt 109 or 110, both of which we know to have been involved in the battle that day. However, more graphic evidence of Klipsch's fate was later noticed in post-excavation research conducted at Farnborough by the air crash investigator Steve Moss. A rifle-calibre (7.92mm) hole in the pilot's door probably marks the entry point of bullet which probably killed Paul Klipsch, causing his Spitfire to fall into its final dive.

Another peculiarity was the recovery of a map box from the Spitfire. This is highly unusual. The map box contained maps bearing the signature of Roger Bushell, squadron leader that day and with whose Flight Klipsch was serving. This is difficult to make sense of. Bushell is recorded as having flown in Spitfire I, N3194, that day. Its fate is unknown, though today it is commemorated at Biggin Hill (**colour plate 19**). Bushell, who baled out, was captured alive and subsequently executed by the Gestapo for his part in the mass break-out from Stalag Luft III. It might be surmised that the excavated Spitfire was his. But we know from identifying marks that it was not the one he flew that day. Then the question must be, had Bushell and Klipsch changed machines? Klipsch's grave nearby suggests he was undoubtedly in P9373, and the recovery of a very small number of human remains subsisting in the wreckage shows that a man certainly died in the crash. It seems probable then that on the day, Klipsch and Bushell had changed machines for whatever reason. Like most archaeological excavations, the dig of a Spitfire leads to new questions in their own right.

Excavating German aircraft

As has already been pointed out, many more German aircraft came to grief over Britain in late 1940 than did British machines. At the time the British press and establishment lost no chance to publicize the incidents, especially if graphic photographs of burning wreckage were available, normally from official sources and suitably treated by the

55 Scrapped Luftwaffe aircraft being prepared for the melting pot in Britain

censors. *War Weekly* of 9 August 1940 featured a typical story labelled 'This Dornier didn't get back' and included three impressive images of the destruction. *War Illustrated* for the same date produced a full-page spread of photographs for the same crash. But censorship meant that neither the incident nor location were readily available to the public (and Germany), and only *After the Battle*'s efforts have traced it to a Dornier Do 17M of 4(F)/14 which came to grief at the hands of No. 238 Squadron on 21 July 1940 at Nutford Farm, Blandford in Dorset. Like so many other downed German aircraft this Dornier was removed to a scrap yard for examination and destruction (**55**). In a small number of instances, the aircraft were retained as flyable examples and were used for evaluation and experimentation.

One peculiarity of the relic trade in Second World War memorabilia is a taste for the iconography of the Third Reich. A casual glance through military magazines and even on the Internet reveals a substantial market in Nazi-associated items that command premium prices amongst collectors (**56**). Amongst the most favoured items are personal effects, weapons and uniforms. The Luftwaffe is no exception and thus this has materially affected the nature of the recovery of some German aircraft in Britain by preferring to seek personal relics of the crew, rather than the machinery. This is also affected by the fact that most of the German aircraft that crashed in Britain had more than one engine. Where a fighter crashes while still in one piece, the engine creates an entry point behind which the fuselage, pilot (if still on board) and his equipment follows behind, compressed into a main block of debris. Multi-engined aircraft tend to break up differently. All sorts of forces are created in a spin into the ground, one of which is to cause the engines to break away from the wings. Even if they remained attached they enter the ground at some distance from the main fuselage. There is of course also the fact that German bombers carried bombs and in some cases crashed before they had dropped their loads. A Junkers Ju 88A

56 *Soldiers carry away a tail fin from Messerschmitt Bf 110C-4 (Wk no. 3113) of I/ZG2 which crashed at Pudsey Hall Farm, Canewdon (Essex) on 3 September 1940. The swastika was later cut from the relic and turned up in an Army and Navy window display from where it entered the collections of* After the Battle *magazine*

of II/LG1 which crashed at The Jumps, West Tisted in Hampshire on 15 August 1940 was one such example, and required attendance by bomb disposal experts to disarm the bombs.

The combination of selective recovery and circumstance tends to dictate what is recovered and how, reflecting some of the conventional archaeological method which forces the excavators to select which part of the site can and will be examined. On 3 September 1940, a Messerschmitt Bf 110C-4 (Wk no. 3113) of 3/ZG2 was shot down by Hurricanes of No. 17 Squadron over Pudsey Hall Farm, near Rayleigh (Essex). The crew had in fact baled out and survived. The aircraft entered the ground with considerable force, so much so that an early excavation of the site in the 1970s located the engines at a depth of nearly 11m. The engines, and many other parts, were left where they were found because it was impossible at the time to recover them. A subsequent excavation in 1986 led to one of the Daimler-Benz engines being extracted. The aircraft is thus an interesting example of one which defied attempts to recover much of it, and it appears that substantial parts of it remain underground. Moreover, it seems that the original crash was widely reported in the press in 1940, featuring a photograph of the local Home Guard proudly displaying one of the tail fins. Remarkably, a section of the fin materialized in the mid-80s and was presented to *After the Battle* magazine. Unlabelled, the fin was only identifiable because of the 1940 photographs and reflected the popularity of acquiring suitably dramatic souvenirs (**56**).

The Pudsey Hall Farm Bf 110 had crashed deep into the ground, thus leaving extensive quantities of wreckage available for post-war recovery. Another example, from 1941, is worth discussing in some detail even though it was not a Blitz or combat casualty. However, the crash was so well documented that it is possible to trace the entire story right through to the extant debris in the Imperial War Museum in London. Had the aircraft not been the one flown by Rudolf Hess, deputy Führer, on the night of Saturday, 10 May 1941, then it would have disappeared into the melting pot like so many others leaving no trace of its crash or of itself in our own time.

The story of Hess's flight is reasonably well known but, briefly, he flew to Britain in an effort to persuade Britain to discuss peace. No-one has ever been certain about the sincerity of the single-handed project. It came to nothing and Hess was imprisoned until his death in August 1987. Hess flew a Messerschmitt Bf 110D (Wk no. 3869, with markings VJ+OQ) which he took from Augsburg. He flew to Scotland, his purpose being to seek out the Duke of Hamilton in hope that he would take Hess's peace mission to the British government. What matters to us is that Hess made no attempt to land. He baled out, and left the Bf 110 to crash at Bonnyton Farm near Eaglesham, south of Glasgow.

Hess's aircraft was scattered widely across the surface, from which it was recovered by an RAF maintenance unit. The *News Chronicle* of 13 May was one of a number of papers to publish photos of the debris on the farmland, while RAF personnel posed. Nothing visible subsists on the site today. It was almost immediately removed to an aircraft scrap yard at Carluke, where it was mixed up with wreckage from other aircraft. At this point, an order was issued to rescue it by the Air Ministry, due to its great importance. The parts which could be identified were transported to London, a journey which seems to have involved removal of portable souvenirs en route. Its fate is unknown because it did not reappear until 1945 in a London hangar. Storage in Shropshire seems also to have been involved. Although photographs exist of soldiers displaying machine guns from it in 1941, none of these has even been located. Today, Hess's Bf 110 has mostly disappeared except for a section of fuselage and an engine, displayed in the Imperial War Museum in London, and the other engine preserved at Duxford, another part of the Imperial War Museum.

On one hand, the notoriety of the occasion might have guaranteed the appropriation of parts of this Messerschmitt. On the other, it is a scarce example of an aircraft which crashed but which was recoverable, and whose fate was recorded. Hundreds of aircraft that crashed in similar circumstances, like the Blandford Dornier, were also removed from the record immediately, but today there is no prospect of examining their physical remains. If we relied on the archaeological evidence we would have a wholly unrepresentative body of data, yet in the case of the air war enough documentation exists to make it possible to compile a full record of most of the events on any given day. It is not stretching the point to consider the fate of ancient arms and armour when distributed across battlefields. Such useful, and recyclable, material was almost invariably recovered if at all possible, leaving little or no trace of what might have been a momentous event. Other battles, such as the invasions of Julius Caesar in 55 and 54 BC, have left no detectable trace whatsoever. Without the historical record we would have absolutely no means of knowing that they had ever occurred.

It is also true that of those aircraft which have been recovered, a substantial amount of dispersal has already taken place. The Rayleigh Messerschmitt was dug by the London Air Museum, a long-dead organization whose effects have disappeared into various anonymous private hands. A Junkers Ju 88A-1 (Wk no. 8095) of 2/KG77 crashed at Folly Farm near Dorking on 27 September 1940, an authentic casualty of the Battle of Britain unlike Hess's machine. The site is reported as having been investigated in 1976, with one engine (port) being removed, which should mean that much of it lies untouched. If the label on a Jumo 211 engine connecting-rod purchased in 1999 is to be believed, then the engine was later subjected to systematic dismantling in spite of the fact that it had been pulled out, with immense difficulty, from a depth of over six metres (**57**). An engine maker's plate from another Junkers Ju 88 which crashed that day was also found circulating on the market, clearly having been removed from the engine casing (**58**).

Tracing two Flying Fortresses

Long after the Battle of Britain and the Blitz, England had become an island of air bases as the air war turned on Germany. The proliferation in hardware and infrastructure is breathtaking, even around 60 years later. East Anglia was covered in bases used by the United States Eighth and Ninth Air Forces to spearhead the daylight bombing campaign. Hundreds of bombers were gathered into massive formations on an almost daily basis to fly over Germany. Holding the formation was vital to navigation and protection. It also generated huge numbers of accidents as four-engined bombers ploughed into one another with catastrophic results. The remains of many of these tragedies lie across eastern England to this day creating a different type of feature.

On 21 February 1944, a B-17G 'Flying Fortress' bomber (serial number 42-31370) of the 385th Bombardment Group of the United States Eighth Air Force crashed in

57 Connecting-rod said to be from a Jumo 211 engine found in the wreckage of Junkers Ju 88A-1 (Wk no. 8095) of 2/KG77 at Folly Farm near Dorking (Surrey). It crashed on 27 September 1940

115

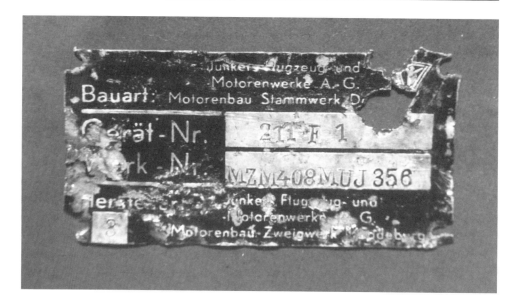

58 Jumo 211 engine plate said to be from the Junkers Ju 88A-5 (Wk no. 0293) shot down by fighters and anti-aircraft fire at Vexour Farm, Penshurst (Kent)

Reedham Marsh (Norfolk), following a mid-air collision with another B-17 (42-37963) of the same group (**colour plate 15**). The incident was one minor tragedy in the greater tragedy of the losses suffered by bomber crews of both RAF Bomber Command and the United States Army Air Force. That this incident was an accident only served to accentuate the sense of waste, made even worse by the discovery that the crew of 42-31370 had completed their tour of duty and would have returned to the USA on completion of the mission. The crashed aircraft fell onto marshland and their contemporary recovery has already been described above.

When the residual wreckage was first noted in the early 1960s by the writer and aviation historian Ian McLachlan there was no immediate evidence for what it had actually come from. One version of local lore had converted the story into the crash of a German aircraft. Only further scavenging amongst local eyewitnesses revealed that a pair of American machines had been involved in a collision, and the approximate location of their crashes. Further trawling in local police records produced information that B-17 Fortresses had been involved, and the date of the disaster. Examination of the land revealed fragments of airframe scattered in the marshland together with mild depressions, reflecting the account of one of the US recovery team that their work had proved extremely difficult.

The combination of documentation which was subsequently traced, and components bearing serial numbers, provided the confirmation of the aircrafts' identities, the names of their crews, and their origin in the 385th Bombardment Group. The eventual excavation work on both sites has taken place sporadically since the mid-sixties and continues to this day. The present author has attended excavations on each machine, conducted in 1998 and

1999. The work revealed interesting aspects of aviation recovery problems not least because of the specific eyewitness accounts of what happened at the time and how this was reflected in the ground. Firstly, both aircraft had broken up partially in the air, as reported by Reginald Mace, working as a marsh labourer in 1944:

> Following the collision several pieces of the plane flew off in all directions. Neither plane appeared to be on fire before the crash, but on crashing each exploded and caught fire.

Three other marsh workers confirmed this:

> Pieces of both aircraft were flying in all directions immediately following the collision until the planes crashed. (AFHRA Roll #46326)

The collision itself was not unusual. The bombers of the Eighth Air Force were flown in extremely tight formation to provide all-round mutual protection. This was exhausting and difficult work which required immense flying skill. It was common for formation discipline to break down for a variety of reasons, complacency on the home stretch being one of them. On the day in question 42-31370 was flown by Captain John Hutchison, on his 25th mission, and 42-37963 by Lieutenant Warren Pease, about halfway through his tour of duty. The journey home from Diepholz was uneventful until the group met thick cloud over East Anglia. They planned to follow the railway line which runs south-west from Great Yarmouth and which pointed directly to their base at Great Ashfield (as it still does). The B-17 pilots were ordered to descend through the cloud in groups of three. Eugene St John was in the third B-17, flying alongside Hutchison and Pease. Many years later he recalled the occasion:

> I pulled in tight with my right wing inside of the Captain's [Hutchison], Lt. Pease flew a bit looser (further out). When we broke through the bottom side of the cloud deck, Lt. Pease was missing. As I looked around for him he broke through under full power directly behind the Captain and descending at a steep angle. As he passed under Hutchison, he pulled up sharply and the rear third of his aircraft wedged between the no. 3 engine and the fuselage of Hutchison's.
>
> The forward two-thirds of Pease's plane broke off and due to the full power he was using, his plane shot straight up and hung there momentarily. At this time I effected a hard left steep turn to avoid involvement. This occurred at 800ft altitude.
>
> My right wing being at a high angle, prevented my seeing what transpired next, but one of my crew stated at a debriefing, that Lt. Pease's plane dropped back down after a prop-hanging stall and sliced through Hutchison's aircraft. Both of course went straight in …
>
> One other thing occurs to me as I think back. As we broke through the undercast and due to our proximity to Hutchison's plane, I could see him

clearly in the cockpit and he had his feet up and was smoking a big cigar;
celebrating the 25th and last of some rough ones.
(Eugene St. John, undated letter)

This exceptionally well-documented accident showed how catastrophic a collision might
be. Both crews were killed outright, the low altitude precluding any possibility of baling
out and surviving. Those who lived until impact would either have been killed by the
force or in the following explosions and fire. In an archaeological sense it was plain that
there would be no recognizable major sub-assemblies except possibly the engines. The
excavation in 1998 on the Pease site produced a scattering of fragments, many of which
originated from the forward section of the fuselage. Large quantities of ammunition and
two machine guns were found. Although the individual components were generally
identifiable as being from a B-17, there was nothing of major consequence to add to the
propeller which had been recovered in the 1970s.

The work had been conducted with a view to introducing conventional archaeological
methods. The consequence was a certain amount of laborious trowelling in marshland
which seemed to ignore the fact that the evidence, such as it was, lay in the state of
components rather than precisely where they were. The marsh was in any case mobile,
and the land could be felt to move when any force was applied through mechanical
diggers. Nothing appeared to subsist at any depth, despite the use of military metal-
detectors.

In fact, the most useful piece of evidence turned out to be the long-excavated propeller.
This was noticed to be feathered. Feathering means rotating the blades (only possible on
a variable pitch propeller) and fixing them so that the thin edge faces the oncoming air.
This is done when an engine is shut down, and prevents uncontrollable windmilling.
Windmilling forces the dead engine to rotate faster and faster until finally the components
seize and the propeller breaks off, usually with devastating consequences as it cartwheels
into the fuselage or an adjacent engine. Interestingly, St John makes no reference to this
though as the event occurred in so short a time it is possible he did not notice. But it raises
the possibility that the accident was caused because Pease experienced engine failure just
as he entered the unpredictable turbulence of cloud and this may have caused him to lose
control. The author's own practical experience of false information supplied by human
senses while flying on instruments was very sobering. It is extremely easy to see why and
how momentary loss of control can occur.

Work on the Hutchison site in 1999 was more profitable (**44**). At the excavation of part
of the wreckage, which the author was invited to witness, one of the four 9-cylinder
Wright-Cyclone radial engines with its propeller was recovered from a depth of
approximately five metres in anaerobic marsh conditions (**59**). It did not provide direct
evidence for the accident but the remains of a very fragmented second engine, together
with another propeller, this time with only two blades left, may well be the engine with
which Pease collided, the missing blade perhaps having been the one which scythed
through Pease's fuselage.

The capacity of a propeller to cut through material was evident during the dig, and it was
plain how under such conditions, slow and delicate excavation would have been fatuously

59 Excavating an engine from the B-17G Flying Fortress (42-31370) of the 385th Bombardment Group in Norfolk marshland involved a great deal of arduous and frustrating work to dig a deep and safe hole

inappropriate. Once exposed, the propeller lay at the bottom of a dangerous mass of semi-liquid mud producing powerful suction. It visibly slid and rotated, sinking further, thus indicating that in any case its present depth was due to gradual slippage in the years following the crash, rather than reflecting its original crash position. The diggers moved quickly, using the bucket of a mechanical digger as support while they lashed ropes to the propeller and then extracted it in a slick and experienced manner, benefiting from the fact that the digger operator had worked on the marshes for decades. Once out, the propeller was safely lowered to firm ground and the engine extracted similarly quickly. Despite having been protected from the atmosphere in the marsh, the magnesium alloy of the engine casing had degenerated so badly during its 55 years under the surface that it had turned into a gravel-like white powder with lumps of a green crystalline form (**15**). Yet other components, such as rubber oxygen masks, clothing, and wood, had survived in almost unaltered form. It was also interesting to see how the explosive nature of the crash had caused dispersal of various components in and around the mud covering the engine before it was extracted.

Perhaps the most prolific find was unfired ammunition, almost invariably as individual items though they were originally stored in belts folded into boxes. This highlights the inherent danger in excavating crashed aircraft. It might come as some surprise to learn that ordnance was often left in crashed wreckage, and this includes unexploded bombs. Bombers taking off which were frequently over-loaded with bombs and fuel were highly susceptible to accidents. Bombers returning from missions were supposed to unload unused bombs over the sea but this did not always happen. In any case, bombers and fighters were almost bound to have unfired machine-gun or cannon ammunition on board. Undisturbed, such material is effectively inert and unlikely to cause harm to anyone three metres or more below the surface of the ground. Brought up to the surface, the ammunition is potentially lethal. Quite apart from the legal proscriptions on handling or removing such items, sheer common sense dictates that it should be disposed of by professionals. A crashed B-17, exposed by the sea on the coast of Kent in 1998–9, was allocated to a recognized recovery group by the Ministry of Defence. Unfortunately, unauthorized individuals dug out the wreckage in advance of the proper excavation, scattering live ammunition which ended up in the possession of local children. At the time of writing the people responsible were the subject of a court case.

The remains of a P-47 Thunderbolt

All the machines described so far had largely buried themselves, apart from Hess's Messerschmitt. None are evident to this day to the layman, apart from the components displayed in museums. The actual sites are almost entirely undetectable. It is therefore worth briefly mentioning one wartime air crash which is still where it lay. In fact it is far from exceptional and there are many other examples. During the war there was a vast need for training, much of which took place in western Britain. Unfortunately, the instruments of the day, the lack of radio beacons and reliable direction-finding equipment, inexperience and poor weather could all easily combine to send a pilot flying straight into a Welsh hillside as he flew east from the Irish Sea.

*60 Airframe from the Thunderbolt (42-75101) lying scattered in forest. See also **colour plate 16***

One Republic P-47 Thunderbolt (42-75101) still lies on the summit of Mynydd Copog near Bala. Based at Atcham (Shropshire), it belonged to the US 495th Fighter Training Group and crashed on 6 May 1944. What makes this crash unusual is that instead of ploughing into the ground it appears to have attempted some sort of forced landing on the relatively flat summit in unknown circumstances. The attempt failed and the aircraft exploded into thousands of fragments which were then widely dispersed across a small area of the hill. Although it was only about a year old (one undercarriage component bears a manufacture date of 18 May 1943), in the circumstances of war this could mean it was already fairly worn out, a condition known as 'war-weary'. Despite the fact that the accident was probably due to altitude and weather conditions, a tired engine and worn controls, together with inexperience, may have played an important part. Today there is no evidence that any of the Thunderbolt ever actually entered the ground, other than superficially. Sheltered by the subsequent growth of pine forest across the site, it has remained there ever since. While the pilot's remains were removed, presumably just after the date of the crash, the rest seems to have been abandoned and forgotten about.

This is hardly surprising. Many other aircraft crashed in the vicinity and fragments of them remain there to this day. Sporadic recovery has resulted in one Merlin engine from a photo-reconnaissance Mosquito being displayed outside a valley farm, but this is unusual (**71**). The Thunderbolt of Mynydd Copog is useful because, apart from what has already been removed, the components illustrate the nature of survival and provide some evidence for the nature of the crash. The Pratt and Whitney twin-row Wasp engine is made of alloy and steel (**colour plate 16**). The alloy components have deteriorated to almost unrecognizable flaking grey-white lumps, while the steel is now solid rust. The steel skinning of the fuselage has survived better under the forest cover and, remarkably, the olive-drab paintwork is still intact (**60**). One substantial piece of twisted undercarriage housing suggests the wheels were lowered when impact occurred, and was twisted when the wheel and its strut were torn out by the rocky surface.

None of the machines described here, even Spitfire I P9373, was special. The Spitfire had been with No. 92 Squadron for eleven weeks, and was only about three months old. Its combat service was combined to a single day. The Fortresses were two of thousands. Nevertheless, they were structurally identical with hundreds of others and an analysis of their fate and how they have been recovered is useful. Their demise symbolizes the fate of thousands of others, and the crews' deaths symbolize the sacrifice made by so many other men and women. It is only right and proper that, 60 years later, we continue to explore the circumstances of their deaths and record our investigations in a way which will help make sense of future digs.

5 The airfields

A casual glance at an Ordnance Survey map of almost any part of Britain reveals a surprising number of airfields. For a small country, the United Kingdom is replete with landing strips, active and redundant, though an older one-inch edition will reveal the sites of many more than are evident today. During the Second World War, dozens were laid out and equipped with buildings and facilities. This is no more apparent than in East Anglia where the proliferation of bases for the American Eighth and Ninth Air Forces during 1942 and 1943 has left an extraordinary amount of evidence for England's time as a land-locked aircraft carrier. Nowadays, that evidence is confined increasingly to a few derelict hangars and huts. The Snetterton (Norfolk) racetrack, once a US bomber base, still bears significant traces of its wartime history, as does North Weald (Essex), an RAF fighter base now sliced in two by the M11 motorway. Andrewsfield (Essex), and Seething (Norfolk), both once American bomber bases with comprehensive facilities including concrete taxi-ways and runways, are now home to light aircraft using just small parts of the areas used in the war. Kenley (Surrey), RAF fighter base and a major target of the Luftwaffe on 18 August 1940, now serves gliders. Conversely, Fowlmere (Cambs), once a satellite station for Duxford during the Battle of Britain, later became home to the 339th Fighter Group of the Eighth Air Force. Today, apart from small sections of roadway it is all but undetectable in the modern landscape.

The fighter airfields of south-east England in 1940 belong to a different class and even a different era to the bomber bases of 1942–5 (**61**). Unlike many of the US bases, they mostly had their origins in the Great War, or even earlier, experiencing various phases of civil or military use in the inter-war years. A few, like Manston (Kent), owed their origins to serving as Royal Naval Air Stations in the Great War. Some were even officially abandoned. In any case, during the Battle of Britain the nature of aerial warfare, the requirements of the aircraft, and the immediacy of the moment were rather different. Spitfires and Hurricanes took off from what were predominantly grass fields and their pilots lived in ramshackle wooden huts, or were even billeted in local houses. Mechanics and other ground-crew were liable to find themselves sleeping in tents (if they got any sleep at all).

Worse, in the early part of the Battle, the Luftwaffe was still concentrating on attacking Fighter Command airfields. The day-to-day trials of operating from primitive facilities and conditions were compounded by bombing raids, the effects of which lingered for weeks or even months. On 12 September 1940, Tony Bartley of No. 92 Squadron arrived at Biggin Hill where the unit had just been posted:

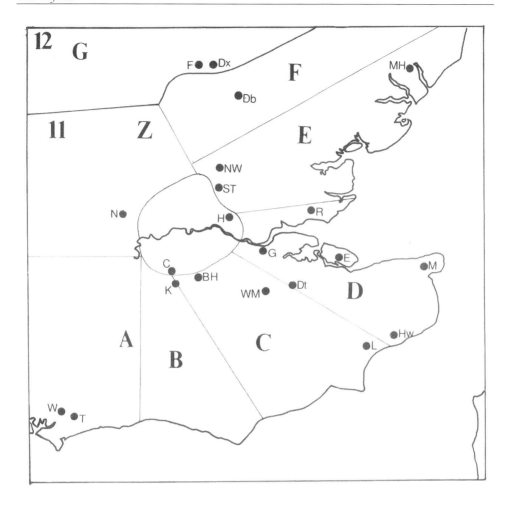

61 South-east England in 1940, showing the main part of No. 11 Group's area of operations, and part of No. 12 Group. Each Group was divided into sectors, indicated by letters. Airfields are: F = Fowlmere, Dx = Duxford, Db = Debden, MH = Martlesham Heath, NW = North Weald, ST = Stapleford Tawney, N = Northolt, H = Hornchurch, R = Rochford, C = Croydon, G = Gravesend, E = Eastchurch, M = Manston, K = Kenley, BH = Biggin Hill, WM = West Malling, Dt = Detling, W = Westhampnett, T = Tangmere, L = Lympne, Hw = Hawkinge

The whole environment was a mess of bomb-scarred earth and bombed-out buildings. The hangars were in ruins, the entire air-field pock-marked with bomb-holes ringed with obstruction warning flags. There were newly laid patches on the runways where craters had been filled in and tarmacked. (Bartley 1984, 34)

62 An unmanned Spitfire of No. 64 Squadron (SH-S) at Kenley surrounded by dust as the raid of 18 August 1940 takes hold. The photograph was taken from one of the Dornier bombers as it flew overhead. Blast from explosions caused the Spitfire to rise up and collapse but was it otherwise protected by the revetments of the blast pen in which it sat

The damage had resulted from raids throughout the second half of August and on into September, an experience suffered by almost all the other airfields. Kenley, for example, a few miles west of Biggin and easily visible from the air to this day as a conspicuous clearing in woodland was almost wiped out on 18 August (**62**). The raids on 30 August were almost as terminal for Biggin Hill (**63**). Oddly though, the extensive damage seems not to have been evident from the air and this explains the continuing raids. A radical local decision was made, therefore, to destroy a hangar that had been rendered unusable but looked intact from the sky.

Later repairs, new facilities, and Biggin's post-war use as a military and then a civil airport, means that there is very little left of the Battle of Britain airfield. Even the commemorative Spitfire and Hurricane which act as 'gate guardians' at the memorial chapel are fakes, reflecting a modern policy of withdrawing aircraft used in this way for restoration, often to flying condition. The Spitfire replica at Biggin today bears the markings of a Spitfire of No. 92 Squadron during the Battle of France, a time when the Squadron was not even based there. Moreover, the replica is in the form of a Spitfire Mark IX or XVI, and thus is entirely inappropriate for the markings (**colour plate 18**).

63 Biggin Hill being bombed on 18 August 1940. The image was recorded by a German aircraft passing high overhead. The airfield had been camouflaged to make it resemble farmland

Other airfields, such as Manston near Margate, have found modern roles as working airfields and, as at Biggin, this has necessarily involved erasing much of their wartime facilities. Goodwood airfield, just north of Chichester, is one of the very few which genuinely resembles its wartime appearance as a grass-field fighter base. Known as Westhampnett in the 1940s, this was once a satellite airfield for Tangmere, east of Chichester. During the Battle of Britain this was home first to the Hurricanes of No. 145 Squadron and, from mid-August 1940, to the Spitfires of No. 602 'City of Glasgow' Squadron. After the war, the airfield's perimeter roadway was used by the landowner, the Duke of Richmond and Gordon, for the basis of what became the Goodwood motor-racing circuit. In 1958 the grass interior was revived as an airfield and to this day it serves light aircraft (**colour plate 17**). Tangmere itself is entirely obsolete and left to its memories (**64**).

But most wartime airfields have simply been rendered redundant. On one hand these have retained more of their original character, but as the twentieth century has given way to a new millennium they have started to disappear with considerable rapidity. By their

64 Hurricanes of No. 601 Squadron at Tangmere in July 1940

very nature then, Battle of Britain and other Second World War airfields are unlikely to exhibit much trace of their part in the summer and autumn of 1940. In the rest of this chapter we will take a closer look at some of the airfields in the frontline and see how they appeared in 1999. The only exception is the armaments and other devices used in defence against attack. As these weapons were used in a variety of contexts they are discussed amongst the other defensive armaments used during the Blitz in the next chapter.

Hornchurch

In 1999 the airfield at Hornchurch in Essex bore a surprising resemblance to its appearance in 1940, though its former function is scarcely evident to the casual visitor. Now called Hornchurch Country Park, the only explicit reminders of its wartime role are the street names which recall some of the more famous pilots who flew from here and other airfields, such as Tangmere Crescent. Closer examination, however, reveals a considerable amount of evidence from the scattered traces of airfield buildings in the soil in the form of brick and concrete fragments right through to pillboxes (**65**) and a virtually unaltered skyline.

Conveniently located close to London and the Thames, Hornchurch was easy for pilots to find and just far enough from the Channel to render it a little less susceptible to

65 Pillbox at Hornchurch. This once stood on the eastern side of the airfield

the regular bombing raids which afflicted Manston, Kenley, Hawkinge and Croydon (amongst others). Its introduction to the air war was swift and bloody when Spitfires were ordered to patrol over the French Channel ports in the closing days of the Battle of France. No. 92 (East India) Squadron, then based at Northolt, arrived daily from 23 May 1940 to use Hornchurch as a forward base. Thereafter, Hornchurch was a major scene of activity throughout the Battle of France and then the Battle of Britain.

Like so many airfields Hornchurch entered the era of aviation as unprepossessing farmland. During the Great War London came under attack by airships which floated ponderously over the conurbation. The Zeppelins carried tiny bombloads totally disproportionate in size to the chaos and terror their forays provoked. In those early days aerial navigation was in its infancy and following the Thames was the simplest way for a Zeppelin pilot to bring his craft over London. Hornchurch's location came to be of the same strategic significance as Tilbury and Gravesend further downriver had been in the days of the seventeenth-century naval wars with the Netherlands.

Sutton's Farm, Hornchurch, occupied by the Crawford family and owned by New College Oxford, became the one of the new air bases in a ring around London. Successes against the airships in late 1916 brought one of the pilots, Lieutenant Leefe-Robinson, a Victoria Cross. In spite of this, the enthusiasm for demobbing in 1918 and winding down war expenditure led to Hornchurch being returned to the Crawford family. This had barely been achieved before the government decided that the site was far too valuable to be restored to agriculture. The eventual arrangements involved farmland being sold to the

66 *Spitfires of Nos. 222 and 603 Squadrons at Hornchurch (Essex). The serials of the machines allow this picture to be fixed in time. XT-M is X4277, the machine in which Richard Hillary (5) was severely wounded on 3 September 1940. ZD-D is X4278, shot down on 4 September, but which had only been allocated to 222 at Hornchurch on 31 August. The photo was thus taken on probably the 1st or 2nd of September 1940*

government while leaving the farmhouse insulated by 300 yards of open land to the north of the putative airfield.

By 1928 the airfield had been opened and in 1929 it was named RAF Hornchurch. During the succeeding ten years, peacetime displays and training prepared air and groundcrew for a war which seemed increasingly likely. By 1938 Hornchurch had been prepared as a Sector Headquarters in No. 11 Group of Fighter Command. No. 11 Group oversaw the protection of south-eastern England and thus inevitably was to face the brunt of the fighting in the Battle of Britain. A fighter airfield of this era was quite unlike a modern airfield. It was essentially an open grass field with a zone to the north-west which contained the main cluster of buildings such as hangars, messes and stores for fuel and ammunition. The field was surrounded with a perimeter road, fortified by pillboxes and barbed wire.

A series of photographs taken on around 1 September 1940 show Hornchurch in full operational mode (66). Remarkably, much of the skyline is unaltered today. Necessarily, the archaeological consequences of operating aircraft from a grass field are unlikely to be very obvious and this is the case at Hornchurch. Although Hornchurch survived as an airfield after the war it was closed in 1962 and became a quarry, while the area used for RAF buildings was built over with a modern housing estate, the boundaries of which approximately reflect the original zone. The back-filling of the quarry has restored a little of the appearance of the original aerodrome but only by elevating the ground level by five metres or more. In any case the growth of bushes and young trees has destroyed any sense of an open grass runway.

In spite of this the site still exhibits some of its original infrastructure. To the west and south, stretches of the perimeter road stand exposed from the scrub, and on the eastern side, close to the stream, the elevated land surface stops abruptly alongside the fighter pens (62) which clustered around the perimeter. These pens consisted of three earth embankments arranged at 90° to create a three-sided enclosure. They enabled aircraft to be dispersed around the field, making it extremely difficult for an enemy to destroy all the aircraft in one sweep. The embankments also prevented blast produced by a bomb from affecting machinery and installations in the less immediate vicinity.

The movement of hardware through an airfield like Hornchurch in war is quite remarkable. The conventional establishment of a fighter squadron was twelve pilots who had access to up to twenty aircraft. Servicing and repairs were taken to account for up to eight of the machines and in theory twelve would always be available. In practice of course this was difficult to adhere to. In late August 1940, No. 603 'City of Edinburgh' Squadron arrived at Hornchurch from Turnhouse (**66**, and **colour plate 10**). Amongst their number was Richard Hillary (**5**), who later recorded their move to the frontline. The first stage in the process was to be summoned from the base at Montrose to the squadron's headquarters at Turnhouse:

> They [the local children] had heard the news and as we went into line astern and dived one by one over the valley, none of the children moved or shouted. With white boulders they had spelt out on the road the two words: 'Good luck'.
> We rejoined formation and once again headed south. I looked back. The children stood close together on the grass, their hands raised in silent farewell.
> (Hillary 1942, 115)

When the squadron reached Hornchurch its induction to the air war was rapid and brutal. Some of the squadrons already based there were in the process of being withdrawn after a brutal series of losses running to up to half the strength. On 28 August four of the members of No. 603 were shot down and three pilots killed, out of about twenty losses for the RAF that day. Although one pilot, F/O I. Ritchie, survived he was wounded and his Spitfire, R6989 XT-X, had to await repairs before being serviceable once more. A single day had seen a loss of a third of the squadron's frontline strength. This was, incidentally, in addition to two Spitfires of No. 54 Squadron (also based at Hornchurch) being lost that day.

The following day, the 29th, Hillary himself was shot down, as was his friend and colleague Colin Pinckney. Both men survived but Pinckney's machine, R6753 XT-G, was wrecked near Dymchurch and would not surface for 36 years (**colour plate 10**). On the 30th two more were shot down, including the squadron leader, George Denholm. Both men survived but their Spitfires, L1067 XT-D (**42**) and R7021 XT-X (again), were lost.

Two more losses for No. 603 Squadron followed on the 31st: X4273 XT-K and X4271 XT-N. The pilot of the former, F/O R.M. Waterston, was killed and the other, P/O G. Gilroy, baled out only to be set upon by civilians in Wanstead who assumed he was German. Remarkably, Waterston's Spitfire crashed in Woolwich and its fragments were gathered and stored in the Woolwich Arsenal. A single Spitfire wing, now at Hawkinge Battle of Britain Museum, is likely to be from this machine but the theory cannot be proved. Gilroy's aircraft destroyed a house, which may have explained his reception committee of belligerent locals.

67 *Spitfire I, P9360, lies on its back at Hornchurch after the raid on 31 August 1940. The propeller boss has been blown off. The raiders did not all get away unscathed* (**22**)

Meanwhile, No. 54 Squadron was sustaining similar casualties. But on the 31st a raid by the Luftwaffe on Hornchurch brought a new type of loss. At least four Spitfires were destroyed on the ground as they tried to scramble (**67**). Other squadrons on the base also suffered losses. No. 222 Squadron lost two.

All this information survives in contemporary documentation and photographs. The wholesale removal of the airfield buildings, and the burial of the grass field under modern spoil, has guaranteed the virtually entire destruction of this major wartime base. It is a reminder that recent history is still susceptible to wholesale erasure, leaving minimal evidence of the airfield's former role even if, paradoxically, the general appearance is not dissimilar. Hornchurch is still an open space, a privilege that one of the other principal airfields of the era was about to lose in 1999.

Hawkinge

In the summer of 1999 the fields that were once RAF Hawkinge were fighting their last battle. Unlike Hornchurch, whose curious fate has left the shape of the original airfield preserved in the landscape, Hawkinge has turned out to be susceptible to a new threat. Only a few miles from Folkestone, and close to the main road to Dover, the old airfield finds itself in a part of Kent exploding with new developments. The local economy has benefited from the Channel Tunnel and the road links to London (the M2 and the M20) have meant that this is a boom area for trade and industry as well as commuting.

Consequently Hawkinge is, at the time of writing, being eaten away by large-scale house building together with a new by-pass (**68**). Much of what remains of the airfield infrastructure is derelict and the Battle of Britain Museum on the site, largely occupying

68 Horses graze beside fields at Hawkinge where once Hurricanes and Spitfires landed. In the distance a modern housing estate begins its inexorable encroachment while archaeologists keep a watching brief

wartime buildings, will eventually end up surrounded by new housing. The present cannot live in the past and Hawkinge has never found a role as a post-war aerodrome in the way that others such as Biggin and Manston have, though it served in the 1968 Battle of Britain film. Nonetheless it is disappointing to see an airfield which had retained much of its 1940 character be subsumed quite so quickly. An archaeological watching brief in 1999 revealed that the site had hitherto unsuspected prehistoric, Roman, Saxon and medieval periods as well.

Hawkinge's origins as a military airfield lie in the Great War when its proximity to the Channel was of vital significance, though the site had earlier been made use of by a Dutch aviation pioneer called Megone. Aircraft of the period had a relatively short range but needed to be flown across to the battlefields of France. The fact that France can be seen from the field will have been an additional factor in an age of primeval aviation techniques. Its undulating contours were not ideal (there is a significant dip in the middle) but this was of less consequence to early aircraft which operated at lower speeds from grass.

Unlike some early airfields, Hawkinge was maintained as a military aerodrome after the Great War. By the mid-1930s Hawkinge had a fairly typical layout of boundaries, with its main buildings and facilities clustered along its north-western boundary. Although this zone has, to a large extent, escaped modern encroachment for the meantime, wartime

69 Dereliction at Hawkinge. A pillbox stands guard while an obsolete airfield-stores building decays to the left. On the right, new homes replace hangars and barracks

destruction and post-war dereliction means that little stands today (**69**).

Hawkinge was initially home to No. 3 Squadron, a Hurricane unit, in the winter of 1939–40 though it did not formally become part of Fighter Command until the early spring of 1940. This was followed by a period of relative calm as the airfield was used for experimentation with remote-controlled aircraft.

It was evacuation from Dunkirk which pushed the airfield directly into the frontline and in the aftermath its defences were rapidly strengthened. Although squadrons were distributed amongst bases, it was normal practice for units to be sent forward to operate for the day from airfields closer to the battle zone. This simply made sense because it meant aircraft were able to operate with freshly-replenished fuel tanks when scrambled. For example, Nos. 32 (**12, 28**) and 610 Squadrons were routinely sent to Hawkinge from Biggin Hill, while No. 64 came from Kenley and No. 501 from Gravesend.

As a frontline airfield Hawkinge was in the thick of the Battle of Britain, being not only liable to Luftwaffe attacks but also acting as an ideal location for crash-landings by RAF fighters which had been damaged or were short of fuel. But, this was also a base for the Boulton-Paul Defiant (**33**). This machine, a two-man fighter, was equipped with a rear-facing turret. Its hopeless susceptibility to an attacker, aware that it could not fire forwards or downwards, was not initially appreciated. No. 141 Squadron was sent to Hawkinge on 19 July, very early in the Battle when such painful lessons were yet to be learned. Scrambled around lunchtime, the Defiant crews were ordered to attack German bombers returning across the Channel. Unfortunately, they were attacked by German fighters which operated the simple tactic of diving and then climbing up towards the underside of the Defiants. Of the nine machines, seven were hit. The pilots of four and the gunners of six were killed. Six machines in total were lost including one that made it back but was written off. The seventh crash-landed. On that day the RAF suffered four other losses, all Hurricanes, with only three of the pilots surviving. No. 141 Squadron was promptly withdrawn and did not return to the Battle until September, and then only for night-fighting out of Biggin Hill.

Major damage resulted to the airfield itself on 12 August 1940. A raid in the late afternoon destroyed the officers' mess, one of the hangars, equipment stores and houses at a time when No. 32 Squadron, then in residence, was away patrolling in north-east Kent. By the time the squadron returned the airfield was semi-derelict. Some of the Hurricanes flew on to Biggin Hill. The others were nearly destroyed in a follow-up attack which wrecked another hangar.

More damage was caused by raids in August, September, October, November and December and continued on into 1941. By the end of 1940 Hawkinge was being used as a base for No. 421 Flight, a new concept in air defence intended to counter low-level German attacks which evaded radar detection. This involved six Spitfires operating initially out of Gravesend, and later Hawkinge. They flew to high altitude and watched out for German raids beginning over France.

Hawkinge's role gradually altered from defensive to offensive. Whereas it had once been essential as a first line in defence, now its proximity to the continent (over which the air war had moved) made it a vital forward base for attacks and also air-sea rescue. Towards the end of the war it once again became a vital defence base against the arrival of the unmanned V1 ('doodle-bug') flying bombs.

The end of the war left Hawkinge with little obvious purpose. It had never been equipped with a concrete airstrip, making it useless for the new jet fighters and bombers. By 1961, after use as a WAAF (Womens' Auxiliary Air Force) training unit and a gliding school, it was closed in 1961. It was this very redundancy though which made it suitable for use in the 1968 film of the Battle and it has thus achieved a kind of celluloid immortality. Even in 1999, in its closing months as a grass field, it retained something of its former atmosphere (**colour plate 19**).

Nonetheless, it is striking how little now exists as detectable features of the wartime airfield. Unlike Hornchurch, where the building sites have long since been built over, Hawkinge might be expected to have retained more obvious remnants of its past. Some pillboxes survive, with one or two even preserved amongst the new houses — a remarkably incongruous image — and scattered remnants of derelict and barely-identifiable buildings. The hangars are traceable now only as overgrown concrete floors, the superstructures having long since been demolished.

But the purpose of the airfield was to support the use of frontline fighters. Of those, no trace now exists apart from the relics gathered in the private museum housed in and around the old watch office building. Perhaps this is the most striking feature of the Second World War airfield. In one sense, the absence of the aircraft is obvious. As flying machines their work was to be in the air and, by their very nature, they were either to end their days in crashes or being scrapped once they were redundant. None of the surviving aircraft of the Battle period seem ever to have flown from Hawkinge.

Perhaps a Roman fort or medieval castle are the only features easily compared. Like an airfield they were designed around a list of basic features and facilities. An archaeologist can expect to find defensive outworks, and the foundations of a series of stereotypical buildings in approximately the same positions. But, like airfields, they were built for the purpose of housing and protecting military personnel and their equipment. Roman forts and medieval castles rarely provide much evidence for the actual business of fighting. Arms and armour are exceptionally rare finds from either context, yet there is scarcely any doubt about their functions.

During the 1999 archaeological watching brief on Hawkinge airfield, virtually nothing was found which would have indicated the purpose of the airfield to an archaeologist, other than its form. Fragments of aeroplanes or servicing equipment were essentially absent and only a small number of practice bombs (used for bomb disposal training) were recovered. This was in spite of scattered artefact evidence for prehistoric, Roman, and medieval occupation (Stevens, forthcoming). In an archaeological sense then, the evidence for the airfield's wartime role is almost non-existent. Were Hawkinge to be levelled today, the only evidence on site which would indicate it was once a wartime airfield (apart from its physical lay-out) would be the graves of the RAF and Luftwaffe airmen that lie in a small corner of the municipal cemetery of Folkestone which abuts the old airfield on its northern boundary. Here, for instance, lies the grave of P/O Charles Woods-Scawen of No. 43 Squadron. On 2 September 1940 he set out from Tangmere (West Sussex) in his Hurricane I, V7420. In a dogfight his machine was set on fire and he baled out near Ivychurch about 12 miles (18km) south-west of Hawkinge. Sadly, he was at too low an altitude and was killed. None of this is evident from his memorial, which is normal (**colour plate 21**).

Thorpe Abbotts

This United States Army Air Force base in Norfolk is interesting to include because although, like many of the RAF fighter bases of the south-east, it has not served as an aerodrome since the war, it has also escaped encroachment from modern buildings and industry. Moreover, it enjoys the facilities of a museum and a preserved control tower (**70**). In this respect it retains a curiously unspoiled aura of authenticity, helped by the large number of derelict structures in the woods and copses which have grown up amongst the ruins.

The fighter airfields, as already discussed, were largely in existence when the war broke out. They benefited from piecemeal and substantial improvements, but damage from bombing and the need to stay operational inhibited complete alterations. However, the new airfields were very much a response to the needs of multi-engined bombers and they required far more in the way of infrastructure to service the needs of dozens of large aircraft and the hundreds of men and women who worked on each base. Just like the machines they were designed to support, they benefited from being designed and

70 *The control tower at Thorpe Abbotts today looking west. The field in the foreground was once a manoeuvring area for B-17 Fortresses of the 100th Bombardment Group*

instigated during the war, by which time it was clear how the war was to be fought. The reasons for this are discussed in more detail in Chapter 6.

From an archaeological point of view these bomber fields are very interesting because they were hasily built, and usually only remained operational for no more than five years and sometimes as little as two or three. It is worth bearing in mind the physical impact of Roman marching camps. Consisting of little more than earthen ramparts and ditches, and perhaps being only used for a single night, many are readily detectable from the air and some can even be seen on the ground.

In order to build the new airfields, land needed to be requisitioned. It was obviously easier and expedient to do this in farmland. As it happens, the agricultural land of East Anglia and Lincolnshire was not only physically suitable but a low density of population and proximity to the North Sea and Europe made it the inevitable choice. East Anglia became the prime location for the USAAF in the form of the Eighth Air Force. Each bomber base required two or more runways. Multiple runways are needed because landing and taking-off need to be executed into the wind to maximise air speed (not the same as ground speed). Cross winds make either activity dangerous, especially when attempting to lift off a bomber laden with fuel and explosives. In practice this means an airfield as an irregular ovoid shape rather more than a mile in length and at least three-quarters of a mile across at its widest point. This area was demarcated by a perimeter taxiway. Clustered around the taxiway were the various dispersals for the bombers, circular hard standings to ease turning, connected by short strips of taxiway to the perimeter road. Beyond this core area all the various buildings such as hangars, bomb stores fuel dumps, messes, hospitals, technical areas, and security, were distributed along a network of service roads up to two miles or more from the actual aircraft.

It is difficult now to appreciate just how much construction work these airfields involved. One estimate has compared the runways and taxiways alone to being the equivalent of 4,000 miles of motorway. The work was done by British contractors as well as US Army units but, regardless of the numbers of men involved, the sheer scale is breathtaking.

Thorpe Abbotts was begun in 1942, and built by a British contractor. Between 1943 and 1945 it was the base for the 100th Bombardment Group, a unit which used the B-17 Flying Fortress (**colour plate 14**). The outfit became notorious when the belief started to circulate that the 100th was experiencing exceptional losses, partly as a result of a perceived German revenge campaign. The latter had developed out of an occasion when a Fortress lowered its undercarriage, considered a sign of surrender, but proceeded to defend itself against attacking fighters. No-one knows the truth — the undercarriage could just as easily have been lowered if the hydraulics had failed — but the story exemplifies the creation of myth in war. Like most other US units, the 100th returned to America in 1945.

The airfield was never used again by the military. Nevertheless, it bears considerable evidence for its wartime role even though the runways have entirely disappeared under agriculture. Despite the length of its main runway, this was still not enough to prevent accidents. On one occasion, overloading of aircraft led to three crashing on take-off and all three crews (30 men) being killed. The area in which the runways once lay still very much resembles its wartime form and it is easy to visualize the airfield's 1940s' appearance. To Harry Crosby, a navigator with the 100th, Thorpe Abbotts looked like 'a small town' when he arrived in May 1943, estimating its population at some 3,000. Like his colleagues he found the purchase of a bicycle essential.

Much of the perimeter track and some of the hard standings have survived, and a stretch of the former has even been integrated into the local road network. To the south, various buildings are crumbling into ruin hidden by the woods. Some, however, like the Quonset barrack huts were made of metal. Generally these have been removed, leaving only the foundations, though at some bases they survive as farm outbuildings. Happily the control tower has been saved from destruction and now forms the centrepiece of an active memorial to the 100th Bombardment Group and other units of the Eighth Air Force.

But like the fighter airfields of the south-east, the aircraft, the very purpose for the fields, are conspicuous by their absence. Few even of their crash sites are marked, though isolated examples exist (**71**). It is left to museums like the Imperial War Museum at Duxford to preserve examples, but these mostly lack any genuine historical authenticity (**colour plate 14**). In the United States and France genuine combat examples survive but, like for example the celebrated *Memphis Belle* and *Shoo Shoo Shoo Baby*, they are heavily restored. Both these machines flew with the 91st Bombardment Group out of Bassingbourn, the former (41-24485) being returned to the United States after completing a tour of 25 missions. It was represented in the 1989 motion picture by, amongst others, the British-based *Sally B* (44-85784) which has no combat history. This machine flies

71 Merlin engine from Mosquito PR.IX, LR412, of No. 540 Squadron. The aircraft crashed into the hillside at Aran Fawddwy (near Bala) on 9 February 1944, killing the crew. The engine is displayed outside a farm at Esgair-gawr off the A494 road about 4 miles west of the crash-site

today, despite enormous mechanical difficulties at the end of the nineties (though at the time of writing, her future is uncertain), in the *Memphis Belle*'s markings.

Shoo Shoo Shoo Baby (42-32076) was interned in Sweden and later converted to airliner use. It then passed to France's *Institute Géographique Nationale* before being abandoned in woodland next to an airfield. At enormous expense and trouble it was returned to the United States, eventually restored to its wartime state in Delaware, and flown under its own power to the Wright-Patterson Air Force Museum, Dayton, Ohio where it now resides. Unlike *Memphis Belle* it is technically airworthy but in practice no such risk will be taken. France's *Lucky Lady* (44-8846), another *Institute Géographique Nationale* machine, not only still takes to the sky but has a combat service record with the Eighth Air Force's 351st Bombardment Group.

Despite the absence of aircraft, the enduring aspects of Thorpe Abbotts, and others like it, bear testimony not only to the colossal efforts expended at the time but also illustrate the process of structural decay. This raises an interesting question of cost which is rarely applied to interpreting archaeological phenomena. Hadrian's Wall is an example of a monumental physical undertaking which obviously used a very large quantity of resources (up to 3.7 million tonnes of stone alone) and an enormous amount of manpower. That the Roman high command ordered its construction is astonishing enough, but its virtual abandonment a generation later is often treated as being somehow inexplicable given that cost. Its subsequent reoccupation might, on the face of it, make this abandonment all the more enigmatic. The fact is though that under circumstances of war (or expectation of war), expenditure is usually almost unlimited. What is needed will be provided. So it was in the Second World War, and when those resources are no longer required then they are simply abandoned or adapted for some other purpose. This was precisely what happened with dozens of similar airfields. And, had the circumstances of the Cold War required otherwise, they would have been recommissioned in the 1950s or '60s had that been considered suitable.

6 The Blitz

Preparations

Despite the ominous warnings from Europe, preparations in Britain for defence against bombing were very much less substantial than in Germany where fully-equipped public air-raid shelters were being constructed long before 1939. The pre-war manufacture date of some equipment, such as gas masks, and the delivery of around 1.5 million Anderson shelters, show that the British government anticipated that civilians would be directly affected but without much idea of what that would actually involve (**72**). Even once war had broken out a series of unseemly rows between national and local government ensued, widely covered in the press, over who was to pay for air-raid protection. If nothing else this provoked disbelief in some quarters that the enemy could be furnished with such detailed information on preparedness or lack of.

Bombing could and did cause an enormous amount of damage and loss of life but it soon became clear that it was nothing like as simple to destroy cities and people as some had imagined. Bombers were far from invincible and command of the air proved rather harder to achieve than expected, especially by day. Nonetheless, this took time to become apparent and when it came to war in 1939, the government's solution was to remove children from the cities believed to be the most likely targets rather than invest vast quantities of money and resources into shelter building. Barbara Castle, the well-known politician who served at the time as an ARP warden, said on a recent radio programme that the evacuation of children was a 'cheap panacea for our lack of preparedness'.

The product of this is that, in an archaeological sense, much of the evidence for bombing as it subsists at the end of the twentieth century is primarily negative. Essentially it consists of the absence and/or replacement of buildings which were destroyed by bombs and, occasionally, scarring of others which remained serviceable and which still stand. Interestingly, very few are now distinguishable as bomb sites without documentary evidence which raises the question of how they would be interpreted without that documentation or photographic evidence. Another intriguing category is the restored or repaired building, with the additional variant of relocated structures. Sometimes this work has been performed so skilfully that it is no longer possible to easily identify buildings that were restored rather than demolished or which were bodily removed to a new setting. There are other peripheral pieces of evidence, such as official air-raid personnel equipment, booklets, and even pictures or other items prepared for the Blitz with strips of gummed paper to prevent the dispersal of broken glass.

72 *Prefabricated steel sheets for Anderson shelters being delivered to London homes for self-assembly or by a contractor in back gardens. Extant versions are often buried under concrete, earth or sand and the metal will not be readily visible. But see* **90**

Bombers

Fears that bombing would begin the moment the war started were given credence by the sounding of air-raid sirens moments after Chamblerlain announced that war had been declared. But the initial moments of panic gradually subsided as it became evident that whatever Germany's plans were, they did not for the moment involve destroying British cities. There were several reasons for this. If we look ahead later into the war we can see that it was only possible for the Allies to sustain a concentrated and devastating bombing campaign against Germany by using a force with a core of four-engined heavy bombers and because the Allies had control of the air. Whether the campaign was decisive or not in bringing about Germany's surrender is not relevant here; what matters is the nature of the hardware which had to be developed.

By 1942 Britain and America had the comparative luxury of being able to design and build new machines in the light of what was required, and to do so in relatively undisturbed airspace. Their factories were not being systematically targeted and their air forces were not being obliged to allocate most of their men and machines to front-line aerial defence. Despite official emphasis on bomber technology in Britain during the

1920s and early '30s, the failure by government to subsidize aircraft design which led to snail's pace development had helped Britain end up having to build for the war in hand and not the one imagined. This is not to say it was a close-run thing; it was, but Britain was not, in the end, hamstrung by fighting with the wrong equipment in the wrong war even if some of the equipment she had at the beginning left a lot to be desired.

The Luftwaffe had always been obliged to operate with compromises. Most of her military aircraft had been devised with parallel civilian roles in order to get away with designing them in the first place. The four-engined Focke-Wulf Fw 200 'Condor' was in production by 1938 as a civilian intercontinental airliner, capable of crossing the Atlantic in one hop. On the face of it, the machine looks if it might easily have been manufactured as a bomber too. But its civilian heritage meant that it was just not strong enough, and despite being capable of carrying a modest bombload it was liable to break its back on landing. Instead it found a more durable role as a long-range reconnaissance aircraft sent out over the sea to spot for Allied convoys.

By 1938 any legal restrictions on German military hardware were academic, and attempts were made to design and build a long-range heavy bomber from the drawing board. The Heinkel He 177 was the result. It was still designed as a twin-engined aircraft but the power requirements were so high that two pairs of Daimler-Benz engines were installed. A number of problems developed. Firstly, the engines proved to be unreliable and prone to fire and, secondly, the structure of the aircraft proved to be weak. By the time these problems were coming under control, Germany could not spare the manufacturing resources or fuel for this type of machine. Although Germany's achievements in developing aircraft and improving production during the war were extremely impressive, resources were increasingly allocated to defence while losses of fuel production from bombing and experienced aircrew made the value of some of the new equipment largely academic.

Britain's Avro Manchester bomber proved a similar disaster. Also using four engines adapted into two, it was plagued by unreliability. But the imaginative and practical solution, replacing the pair of Vulture engines with four Merlins and calling the result the Lancaster, came in a wholly different context of air supremacy and a longer-term strategic initiative. In Germany there had never been any serious expectation of such a protracted and widespread conflict, something which the high-speed fall of France in 1940 had made an entirely credible prospect, and some of the equipment reflected this. The Junkers Ju 87 (Stuka) dive-bomber worked effectively when there was no serious opposition (**10, 16**). Douglas Bader called it 'the easiest enemy aircraft in the war to shoot down' (1973, 25). High losses meant it lasted no later than 19 August in the Battle of Britain and was withdrawn, eventually finding a role on the Russian Front.

In practice, therefore, Germany confronted 1940 with no operational four-engined heavy bomber force and no serious prospect of one in design and production (**73**). When Hitler ordered the bombing of British cities, the Luftwaffe was obliged to do so without the right equipment. In any case, by the end of the year she had lost control of the airspace by day and was coming under pressure at night. Britain's own bomber force was being developed with more heavyweight equipment, dating back to an Air Ministry specification and Defence White Paper of 1936 which prioritized medium and heavy bombers. The

73 A pair of Dornier Do 17 bombers track north-west towards London over the Thames on 7 September 1940. These twin-engined machines were a staple part of Germany's bomber force. The aircraft in the centre is directly over what is now known as Thamesmead. North is to the upper right

four-engined Stirling (**74**) and Halifax models entered RAF service in late 1940, with the ill-fated Manchester following before it was replaced by the brilliantly-successful four-engined Lancaster in 1941–2. Air crew were trained in the peaceful skies over Canada, the USA, and in southern Africa, while the Dominions furnished almost 40 percent of all RAF aircrew between 1939–45. These men bombed by night while America's Flying Fortresses and Liberators filled the daylight bombing skies.

Nonetheless, it was an agonizing process. The Stirling could not fly high enough to be effective. The Halifax was initially plagued by design defects. The early version of the Boeing Flying Fortress bought by the RAF turned out to be ill-equipped to function properly at the high altitude it was designed for. American forces did not really start to come on stream until late 1942. But the point really at issue is that the problems were largely overcome by mid-1943 through working on the war in hand, rather than a war anticipated, a luxury Germany did not have.

74 *Bombing up a Stirling c. 1940–1. Despite the small wing-span which inhibited this model's performance, the sheer scale of a four-engined bomber of this era is apparent from the size of the maintenance crew members swarming across it*

The Blitz begins

Overall then, Germany suffered from almost all the disadvantages she possibly could have done once she engaged in a protracted bombing campaign. Bombardment of British towns and cities did not begin in earnest until late 1940, once the daylight attacks on RAF bases gave way to the night bombing which characterized the Blitz. The initiation had been an accidental bombing of London on 24 August when a Luftwaffe force lost its way to their oil refinery targets and dumped their loads over London. The retaliatory bombing of Berlin over the next ten days by the RAF acted as a catalyst to Hitler's mercurial decision-making process. He promptly abandoned his plan that London would be left unharmed in preparation for his triumphal march down Whitehall, and instead ordered bombardment to punish the British, draw Fighter Command out in their droves to defend the capital and thus occasion the Fall of Great Britain.

These raids differed day by day, dictated by the selection of individual targets, the available hardware and the weather. It would also be wrong to create the impression that bombing was exclusively transferred to the hours of darkness. On 26 September 1940, for example, the Supermarine works at Woolston and Itchen (Hants) were severely damaged in a daylight raid. The result was a significant temporary decline in supplies of the Spitfire I. Had this event occurred much earlier then the consequences could have been drastic. But it was too late in the progress of the Battle; the invasion had been abandoned and the shortfall was happily made partly good by the new Castle Bromwich plant building the Spitfire II. Another consequence was an increase in the amount of dispersed manufacturing processes amongst a multitude of small businesses in southern Britain.

The German high command had given up hopes of Britain's early capitulation and resorted to punitive measures against the general public. On 1 November 1940 alone, raids hit London, Birmingham, and Coventry, while attempts were made against Portsmouth and Southampton. Two weeks later Coventry city centre was practically annihilated on the night of 14/15 November. On 29 December an enormous raid on London produced not only a firestorm but also the celebrated photograph of St Paul's surrounded by flames and smoke (**75**). The night of 21-22 March 1941 involved a similarly devastating assault on Plymouth and Devonport which wrecked or damaged 18,000 houses and killed more than 300. But these are only instances in a sustained, and almost nightly, campaign. The crushing impact which a few night raids could have is illustrated by Manchester's fate on the nights of 23 and 24 December 1940. The two nights resulted in 376 deaths, a number which exceeded one-third of the total in the city for the whole war.

It was not unusual for the Luftwaffe to experience minimal losses on its new night raids, emphasizing the change in the character of the air war with consequences for the archaeological record. The Coventry raid of 14/15 November 1940 cost the Germans just one bomber. Douglas Bader had taken off 'eagerly' with two colleagues of No. 242 Squadron to confront the threat. Neither he nor his colleagues 'saw a thing except fires and gun flashes below' (1973, 131). On the night of 28-29 April 1941, 145 aircraft were sent to bomb Plymouth and Portsmouth. Claimed victories for the night seem to have amounted to six, though it is unclear from accounts whether the actual losses exceeded two.

The reason was, very simply, that the Spitfire and Hurricane were hopelessly unsuitable for night fighting, though some pilots scored astonishing successes in the most unlikely conditions. Locating enemy aircraft in the dark (and identifying them) was hard enough but the exhaust stubs, just ahead of the pilot's position, produced blinding glare. The Defiant, which had proved so tragically unsuitable in daylight combat, made good some of these deficiencies by having a rear-facing turret and a gunner. He could guide his pilot to a position just forward and below a bomber from where he could aim at its underbelly unobserved. But this was a compromise, dependent on visual sightings, and the Defiant lacked speed and a choice of armament.

The eventual result was the development of dedicated night-fighting aircraft, primarily the Bristol Beaufighter which came into service in late 1940 (**76**). Delays caused by bombing damage to the factory at Filton meant that it did not become truly effective until 1941. Twin-engined, heavily-armed, and equipped with radar, this two-man machine was used in conjunction with anti-aircraft fire from the ground to attack night bombers. The night of 19/20 November 1940 was the occasion of the first recorded success with the new

75 *St Paul's surrounded by fire at the end of December 1940. In the flames around the cathedral,
many of Wren's lesser works as well as offices and business were being consumed*

76 *The Bristol Beaufighter I, fitted with radar, four cannon and six machine guns which supplanted
the make-do efforts of adapted fighters and Blenheims*

Beaufighters. A Junkers Ju 88A-5 (Wk no. 2189) of 3/KG54 was hit by a Beaufighter of No. 604 Squadron over central England though in fact the machine struggled south to crash near East Wittering (West Sussex) with two of the four-man crew surviving. But the fact is that numbers brought down on a daily basis were minimal compared to losses which had been inflicted in the daytime during the Battle of Britain.

Weapons

Contrary to the popular image of large high-explosive bombs dropping out of the bottoms of German bombers, much the most significant weapon was the incendiary bomb (**77**). The laying waste of large tracts of British cities testified to the effectiveness of dropping vast numbers of incendiaries (weight for weight, some five times more effective than conventional explosive) at night. This was of crucial importance, considering the limited bomb-carrying capacity of a German twin-engined bomber of the 1940s.

A remarkably crude weapon, the incendiary exploited the properties of magnesium, the same properties which complicated its use in aircraft parts and which caused its rapid disintegration. The basic incendiary device weighed 1kg or 2kg and consisted of a cylinder of magnesium with a central core of thermite (a highly-combustible compound of aluminium and iron oxide), fitted with a flush steel tail and an explosive device in the head. The explosive was intended merely to start a small fire which caused the magnesium

77 *Incendiary bombs. The complete example, a 1kg Type B1E, is said to have been dropped on the airfield at West Malling (Kent) in August 1940. Its date of manufacture, 1936, can be discerned on the body. Disarmed, it was donated to a local member of the Home Guard in 1940. Length 348mm. The tail unit is from another example said to have been dropped on Klingers Factory, Sidcup (Kent), in 1940. In this case the fins have been scarred as the magnesium alloy of the bomb's body burned*

and thermite to ignite. At this stage they could be easily put out with a bucket of sand. But, once ignited, the bomb could burn for three to four minutes. Unattended, this was time enough to utilize the potential energy in the materials which went to make up a building, often by setting wooden rafters or furniture alight. Peter Elstob recalled a night racing around trying to extinguish them. He encountered a hysterical woman screaming that her mother was dead.

> The incendiary had crashed through the roof and the bedroom ceiling, landing on the bed. All the smoke in the house was coming from the burning mattress and bedding. The bomb had long since burned itself out and the spray soon had the fire out. As the smoke cleared we could see an old lady in the bed. She was quite dead.
> Once outside again we were grabbed by a little old man in a white muffler who begged us to put out some incendiaries lodged in his attic. We got these out fairly quickly but then he pointed to a ladder and an open skylight, saying there were more on the roof . . .

But the purpose of the incendiaries was not only to start fires of destruction. They acted as beacons too.

> I started to spray the incendiary lodged by the chimney when I heard the sound of more bombs coming down and hugged the peak of the roof. Moments later a stick of small, 50-pound high explosive bombs fell in a line across houses and street.
> The bombers, earlier in the evening, had dropped nothing but hundreds of incendiaries. But this wave, a couple of hours later, came back with instantaneous high-explosive bombs where the fires were brightest and most people were in the streets. (Elstob 1973)

High-explosive aside, it did not take long for a load of incendiaries to start a destructive conflagration which could leave large parts of a city centre in ruins by morning, however hard people tried to put them out. Thermite, for instance, burns at a temperature of around 3,000°C. Incendiaries were not, in fact, especially reliable as individual bombs but the sheer numbers dropped could virtually guarantee a fire of sorts. They could be packed into containers holding up to 700 units. Today there is no more potent memorial to their effect than the ruins of Coventry cathedral (**78**, and **colour plate 25**). Only the steel tails of incendiaries which worked normally survive and these show traces of the burning, and the magnesium of the bodies (**77**).

Fire was so potent a weapon in aerial bombardment that it is not surprising there were other methods. There were many variations on the incendiary, and these include more conventional-looking bombs that had incendiary fillings, including an exceptionally unpleasant model called the *Phosphorbrandbombe*. As the name implies, phosphorus formed part of the filling but was kept separate in glass containers. These shattered on impact which allowed the phosphorus to mix with oil and rubber in the rest of the casing. The

78 *The gutted nave of St Michael's cathedral church in Coventry after the terrible night of 14/15
November 1940. The entire superstructure has been destroyed. See **colour plate 25** for its
present state. Post-war reconstruction involved the demolition of the houses in the background for
road-widening*

resultant spreading and burning liquid could cause horrific injuries to anyone unfortunate enough to be covered by it.

Other bombs formed variants on basic high-explosive types and were known as SC bombs. Right up to the present time, and doubtless long into the future, examples of these have continued to turn up on building sites. As recently as late October 1999 an area of Reading town centre had to be cleared after yet another was exposed. Of various weights from 50kg to 2500kg, these contained TNT and other explosives like amatol (made of ammonium nitrate and trinitrotoluene). The explosion was set off by an electrical or mechanical fuse that either operated on impact or was set with a time delay. In fact, some models were equipped with a ring that was supposed to inhibit burial and make sure the explosion occurred on or close to the surface. The Luftwaffe also dropped aerial mines, and armour-piercing bombs, but these were primarily intended for destroying enemy shipping or military fortifications. Mines were supposed to be dropped in shipping lanes where they were supposed to wait until the proximity of a ship would set off their magnetic or acoustic detonation equipment. But, being also designed to explode on accidental impact with dry land (to prevent their mechanisms being dismantled for analysis), they could also cause major damage to buildings. This led to their intentional use on land-based targets during the Blitz with such devastating effect that immediate moves were made to censor any publicity about them.

Defences

Radar was in its infancy in the 1930s and '40s but it was sufficiently effective to provide Fighter Command and civil defences with a warning that a raid was imminent, and roughly which direction it would come from. Using a system of stations around the east and south coasts it was possible to fix an approximate distance and direction of incoming aircraft, and to make an estimate of the strength of the force. Not unnaturally the stations were targeted during the Battle of Britain. For example, the station at Poling (West Sussex) was attacked by Stukas just after 2.15pm on 18 August 1940, with 44 bombs impacting on the site. Barely 16 minutes before, the station had been one of several to detect the approach of enemy aircraft. Warnings were essential, but radar did not destroy aircraft. The most obvious features of these stations were their steel-girder (and some wooden) towers, as high as 360ft (110m). Naturally, they have long since been redundant and safety has forced their demolition and removal, apart from one example at Stenigot near the Lincolnshire coast which survived for a long time in use for climbing training. With these gone, generally the only surviving evidence is in the form of blockhouses.

Apart from the fighters scrambled to meet them, there were other devices designed to detect and destroy individual machines.

Light and sound locators
Defence against night bombers was largely futile without searchlights. Ground-based guns were ineffective, fired randomly, but lights could also pick out friendly aircraft which were then shot at too. Mobile searchlights with their own generators used electric arcs to

*79 A mobile sound locator.
See text for explanation*

create a very bright light which was concentrated into a parallel beam with reflectors contained within the light housing. To keep the light constant the carbon filament was rotated. Burning at around 3,000°C, the main problem was heat which had to be dispersed.

The searchlight was used in conjunction with a mobile sound locator. This curious looking device was fitted with four cones designed to capture sound (**79**). One crew member listened to the output of two cones A and B, tracking the movement of an aircraft from left to right by finding the direction in which the sound was strongest. Another crew member listened to the output of cones C and D to find the elevation. The parameters were established and transferred to a searchlight which would then, hopefully, pick up the intruder and illuminate him. Sound location had, of course, one huge disadvantage compared to radio-detection, which supplanted it. The speed of sound is sufficiently slow to mean that an enemy bomber flying at 240mph at 20,000ft might actually be a mile ahead of where its sound appears to emanate from. Fixed sound-receiving installations also existed. Close to the present-day airfield at Lydd (Kent) is a large curved concrete acoustic wall facing across the Channel towards the German airfields of the Pas de Calais area. It remains a conspicuous monument in today's landscape.

Guns

In some respects the provision of anti-aircraft guns seems virtual folly. Shooting down bombers lit up by searchlights might very well lead to aircraft crashing on built-up areas. It was in any case extremely difficult to identify and shoot down a fast-moving piece of machinery at altitude in broad daylight let alone in the middle of the night, and shells which missed their target were liable to fall to earth in unsuitable places. Worse, the machine shot down might turn out to be British. Nonetheless, it was psychologically important to provide tangible evidence of retaliation and retribution though the noise could be more annoying. Tony Bartley recalled how the 'gun battery kept up its infernal racket all night long' (1984, 52).

Oddly, gun technology was less prone to development and improvement than other aspects of modern warfare in the 1940s. The Bofors gun, which fired 40mm 2lb explosive shells, was an effective weapon but there were too few available to have the desired effect. It was also only really suitable for defence against low-level attacks on airfields. The 3-inch guns designed and used in the Great War were still widely in service in 1939, though large numbers were lost with the British Expeditionary Force in France in June 1940. The replacement was the 3.7in Vickers gun designed in 1936 and mounted on a rotating plinth designed to be mobile for army use. The 28lb (13kg) shells could reach an altitude of 30,000ft but in practice they were not effective beyond 18,000ft, but this was about 4,000ft better than the old 3in guns. A larger, 4.5in gun was just available by 1940 but its shells weighed just under 86lb (40kg) and it was not suitable for mobile use.

The lower the altitude the faster an aircraft would cross the gun's effective zone of attack, and the more quickly any information from a sound locator or searchlight would become useless. The method involved firing at where the aircraft would be when the shell got there. This relied on an accurate estimate of the machine's speed, height and direction. Gun emplacements therefore needed range-finders, predictors and operators for them to achieve this. Shells carried clockwork mechanical fuses and these needed to be set to blow the shell up at the right height. The higher the aircraft, the less effective the shell. In any case, guns could not be installed everywhere and consequently it was possible for waves of bombers either to avoid as many as possible or to fly high enough to minimize the risk. The main locations were around the principal ports like Dover and Portsmouth, and also along the Thames Estuary up to and around London. Naturally, these guns do not survive in place. Most had operational potential right on into the 1950s and were thus simply removed, reused, stored or scrapped after the end of the war.

It will of course be quite obvious that if anti-aircraft fire succeeded in damaging or downing an enemy aircraft there was no means of controlling where it crashed. In an ironic twist, it was anti-aircraft fire that indirectly occasioned the first civilian deaths of the air war in Britain. In the late evening of 30 April 1940 a Heinkel He 111H-4 was flying over the sea off East Anglia, engaged in mine-laying operations. The crew lost their way in fog but when they broke into a clear patch they were immediately spotted off the Suffolk coast. The resultant barrage of fire seems to have damaged the aircraft, which then headed south over Essex, steadily losing height until it hit housing in Victoria Road, Clacton-on-Sea. With such a shallow gradient the aircraft carried on for several yards, crossing the road and demolishing houses before one of its mines exploded. Incredibly, apart from the crew, only two people were killed but 156 were injured (**13**). This was partly due to the fact that the crash attracted attention and just enough time elapsed for people to accumulate in the vicinity. Little or no trace of the occasion survives today but at the time it was a sobering discovery that defence could lead to such tragedy.

On 1 November 1940, anti-aircraft fire gained another success with a Heinkel He 111P-2 (Wk no. 1571). The aircraft crashed in back gardens in Hornchurch, two of the crew of four having baled out. It seems to have been fuel from the machine that caused a large fire in the back gardens, killing at least one entire family in their Anderson shelter. Conversely, another incident did for the aircraft and crew but with no civilian casualties. A Junkers Ju 88 (Wk no. 5151) was one of eleven machines despatched from I/KG76 at 2155 on the evening of Saturday, 19 April 1941. At 2230 it was shot down by anti-aircraft fire from guns at Brooklands. It crashed near Slinfold, West Sussex, killing the whole crew. The wreckage was partly recovered in recent years (**80**).

A novel variant of firepower was the parachute-and-cable device. These were useful for defending airfields but only up to about 600ft. They were also only really effective in daylight. When aircraft approached rockets were fired, towing 480ft of steel cable. When the rocket was spent a parachute opened and the cable slowly dropped into the path of the oncoming bomber. If the bomber hit it, the force broke the cable away from its mooring, pulling out another parachute. The result was a heavy cable snagged around the aircraft which forced the pilot to lose control as he fought against the drag effects of the two parachutes. Difficult though it may be to believe, the parachutes could produce very much more braking than the engines could counter. The result was a loss of enough air speed to sustain lift and the aircraft simply fell out of the air.

On 18 August 1940 a number of these devices were positioned on the north-west side of Kenley and were used against the raid by Dorniers that day with variable success. One machine was struck as it was in a bank at the time the cable slipped off the wing, and control was regained. Another, a Dornier Do 17Z-2, was brought down, killing all the crew, but the aircraft crashed into a nearby house. This was remarkably bad luck but no civilian casualties were reported. Cables also served as static anti-landing devices. Using an A-frame tubular support on either side of a road, a heavy steel cable could be strung out across just high enough to rip the undercarriage off any aircraft intending to put down there. This was, however, specifically an anti-invasion device.

The author had cause to appreciate the implications of being hit by a parachute-and-cable device when an aerial cable on his Cessna snapped. Despite being only a flimsy piece of narrow-gauge wire it flailed around in the aircraft elevator surfaces causing turbulence and drag and raising the very real risk of losing control. After an emergency landing the damage to the rudder was plain from the smearing of the paintwork, a sobering pointer to what might have happened with thicker cable.

Balloons

The barrage balloon provided a similar defence to the parachute-and-cable. These blimps had internal hydrogen bladders and were nearly 19m in length. Attached to cables they were allowed to rise under control of a winch, which allowed an altitude of up to 5,000ft to be reached (**81**). The hydrogen took the balloon up, and the bladder expanded as the air

80 Piston and con-rod from one of the Jumo 211 engines fitted to the Junkers Ju 88 (Wk no. 5151) of I/KG76, shot down at 2230 on 19 April 1941 by anti-aircraft fire at Brooklands. It crashed near Slinfold (West Sussex)

pressure decreased with altitude. This expelled the air from the body of the balloon, except for the fins which remained filled with air. Leakages of hydrogen could be replenished up a special flexible pipe. The only physical remnants of the balloons are the traces of mooring points though these are unlikely to amount to more than markings in grassland. One is detectable in Greenwich Park close to the Maze Hill entrance.

The advantages of the barrage balloon system were that it lasted as long as the balloons stayed aloft and their reasonable altitude which inhibited bombers from taking low-level (and more accurate) bombing runs. Part of the secret of their success lay in the technique of distribution. Obviously not everywhere could be covered. A bomber flying through a screen of balloons had only to risk them once. But where a bomber flew into a field of balloons, the chances were much higher that his track would lead him to collide with one eventually.

Balloons were reasonably mobile and only needed to be hauled down, deflated and moved to a new site on the back of a special truck, though permanent sites were also installed. The system was more sophisticated than the parachute-and-cable. Explosive devices were set off when an aircraft hit the cable and the bomber found itself briefly towing a cable and two parachutes before it crashed.

Unfortunately balloons were susceptible to being shot down and could be dangerous to friendly aircraft which had strayed, especially at night. This was made even more dangerous when balloons broke away from their moorings. It is important to remember that there was a vast amount of daily and nightly aviation traffic over Britain in addition to the activities of Fighter Command. Bomber Command had its own machines engaged in raids on the Continent which obviously had to leave and return. Other aircraft were being used for training and there were many others which were in the process of being ferried

81 Barrage balloon moored over Kensington. The Albert Hall and the Albert Memorial fix the location

GB 8413b
Nur für den Dienstgebrauch
Bild Nr. 780b/40-016 (v.) (Lfl. 3)
Aufnahme vom 3. 9. 40

Stafford
Werk für schwere elektrische Maschinen
„English Electric Co. Ltd."
Länge (westl. Greenw.): 2° 06′ 10″   Breite: 52° 47′ 50″
Mißweisung: — 11° 43′ (Mitte 1940)   Zielhöhe über NN 90 m
Maßstab etwa 1 : 8 300

Genst. 5. Abt.   April 1941
Karte 1 : 100 000
GB/E 16

500   0   500 m

82 *German reconnaissance photograph of Stafford showing the location of the English Electric*
Company. The image is about 2.5 km wide and 2.3 km high. Dated 3 September 1940 and
published April 1941. These images, and those taken by the RAF, provide vital information for
modern archaeologists and surveyors interested in changes in the landscape/

about from manufacturers to their new bases, or being transferred between squadrons. Worse still, it was easily possible for an enemy aircraft, disabled by hitting the balloon, to crash on a residential area just as it was for those shot down by anti-aircraft fire. A Heinkel He 111 of 8/KG27 (Wk no. 2670) crashed in Newport (Gwent) on 13 September 1940. In the impact two local children were killed. Ironically, on the night in question this was the only German aircraft lost over Britain. The German response to the balloons was not only to shoot them down where possible or simply avoid the areas, but also to try installing devices for protecting bombers. One installation involved fitting a framework around the nose of a bomber which was supposed to deflect the cables, but it is of course impossible to assess the effectiveness of such a precaution apart from the fact that it made the bombers so fitted more difficult to control.

Targets and aiming

Figure **82** shows a Luftwaffe aerial photograph of Stafford, compiled to show the precise location of the English Electric Company's plant. Aerial reconnaissance for the military goes back to the earliest days of ballooning, but by the Second World War it had become far more sophisticated. Both sides used specially-adapted models of aircraft to fly at high altitude where they were beyond visual and electronic detection. Fitted with high-resolution cameras the aircraft could bring back immediate and up-to-date images. However, it was also possible to use pre-war photographs, photographs taken earlier in the war, commercial maps, and other material available in the public domain.

The Stafford photograph was taken on 3 September 1940, but was prepared for use the following April. It is only a single example, but thousands of others survive, together with carefully marked maps labelled Zeilgebeit ('Target Area') on which factories, power stations and other significant targets were outlined. Despite this careful preparation it became obvious early in the war that accuracy on the scale envisaged by planners and aircraft designers was simply not possible.

Even finding the target was a problem. In our own time, exact navigation is feasible by using satellite-tracking devices. However, private pilots and yachtsmen still rely on what they can see, estimates and approximations, and spend much of their time compensating for all the variables inherent in negotiating the natural environment of the earth by the simple precaution of looking out of the window. There is no need to enter into the details here, but it is worth bearing in mind that the aviator of the 1940s depended on accurate reading of a compass, as well as taking into account magnetic variation (caused by geographical location, and by the other machinery in the aeroplane), and drift caused by crosswinds. The slightest inaccuracy becomes magnified as the miles are travelled, and a bomber squadron could easily find itself 20 miles from the target. It is easy to see why night bombing was erratic, random, and merciless in its victims.

The use of radio beacons was developed to make navigation more reliable. The transmission of two signals from known locations allowed a navigator to fix the direction of each, plot two lines and mark his position. Similarly, beams could be made to cross directly over the target. In practice, phantom targets (created by installing misleading lights on the ground), interference, jamming, and imprecision of measurement meant that this was far from absolutely reliable. It was possible for the British even to 'bend' signals so that the crossover point was moved over an innocuous area of farmland. But, failure to jam the signals on the night of the 14/15 November 1940 led to the devastating consequences of the raid on Coventry. When the system worked it only took a few bombers to start fires before the later waves were able to see their target easily just from the flames. When it went wrong bombs could fall uselessly over farmland. The HMSO booklet *Front Line 1940–1941* even allocated a whole chapter to this aspect of the Blitz, describing amongst other incidents the dropping of incendiaries on a sheep farm in Somerset on the evening of 3 January 1941. On this occasion Bristol was a major target and the result was a great deal of damage to commercial and residential parts of the city. Despite it being a largely cloudless night it seems that some of the aircraft crews were uncertain of the way and that the damage suffered by the farm was due to one of these strays.

Ideally, the navigator would use a combination of every piece of information he had to hand. The daring daylight raid on Kenley of 18 August 1940 involved the Luftwaffe pilots relying on landmarks such as railway lines and tunnels as well as compasses and protractors to find their way. Under such relatively ideal circumstances, in spite of the losses caused by the defences at Kenley (at least nine Dornier Do 17s were destroyed or damaged in the attack), it is not surprising that a significant amount of damage was caused.

But an airfield is a big place. Kenley is easily identifiable from the air today, surrounded by woodland a few miles west of the equally conspicuous Biggin Hill. Picking out a specific building was quite another thing. The size and openness of an airfield allowed clear bomb runs, so some major damage to the facilities at Kenley was almost inevitable. Bombing towns and cities by day was considerably more complicated even if the trade-off was fewer losses. At night this was compounded even with accurate use of beams. The blackout confounded chances of precisely identifying the target and where the wrong buildings were set alight this simply had the effect of attracting more bombers to the wrong target. As the bombs fell, so they were affected by their own residual forward momentum and drift caused by crosswinds.

Naturally, these phenomena and their effects were fully recognized; the problems were shortcomings in bomb-aiming equipment and imprecision in data available in the heat of the moment. Altitude, for example, is an essential component in the calculation because released bombs continue to drift forward as they fall. Altimeters work by measuring air pressure but they rely on being set for a particular value. Normally this is sea-level pressure in the region the aircraft is flying in, or the pressure at ground level at a selected place. Pressure varies constantly, in time and space. Both rely on the provision of accurate up-to-date local information, hardly forthcoming to a passing bomber navigator. A pilot passing from a high pressure area to a low pressure area while attempting to maintain the same altitude reading will in fact gradually lose height. This is because he is effectively following the pressure, rather than altitude. If it seems obvious that he ought to realize that he is descending, nothing could be further from the truth. A phenomenon in flight is to have little sense of movements up and down when visibility is impaired by cloud or darkness. It is difficult to detect minute changes in up or down movement even on the gyroscopically-controlled artificial horizon. There are simple techniques for predicting the problem. In the northern hemisphere, a law of meteorology (Buys Ballot's Law) is that if the wind is behind you the low pressure is to your left. Thus an aircraft heading north from France to Britain and which is experiencing wind from its left (evidenced by right drift), is demonstrably heading from high to low pressure.

When the situation occurs where a pilot is lower than he planned to be the bombs dropped will hit the ground sooner than expected and probably fall short of the target. Another, human, factor with similar consequences was creep-back. As a bomber stream approached the target, the one thing preying on the minds of all the crew was to make as a fast a getaway as possible. This naturally encouraged them to drop their bombs sooner rather than later. As the lead aircraft started to let its load go so those behind tended to follow suit. Consequently, bombs were dropped progressively shorter and shorter of the target.

The consequence of all this was that the German bombers were ordered either to bomb a zone or area, which they called a Zielräum (literally, an 'aiming district') or, if weather conditions and a bright ('bomber's') moon permitted, targets like a government building complex or a dock. In practice bombs fell where they fell and a bomb aimed at Battersea Power Station was almost as likely to fall on Clapham High Street. Of course, the colossal fires caused by incendiaries made London an especially easy place to find and the meanders of the Thames, manifested as a black snake in the conflagration, made target finding simpler than it might have been. Consequently, large districts like the docks in the East End, or Woolwich on the south bank, were particularly vulnerable. On the other, the plotting of bombs on maps of less-intensely bombed areas during and after the war can often show the track of individual aircraft. As a bomber dropped its load, so the bombs fell in a line along the direction in which the aircraft was flying. A plot of Putney, for example, shows several tracks north-eastwards in the very approximate direction of the bridges (road and railway). One such track runs across Putney Heath, hardly a plausible target, and it seems likely that the aiming point was supposed to be one of the bridges, or perhaps the railway station which lies on the same alignment. Other scattered bombs across the Heath and Wimbledon Common to the south also testify to the inherent inaccuracy and wastage.

Shelters

The most overriding characteristic of air-raid protection was private input. Mass shelters were not provided by the state, and the use of London's Underground train system was a practical solution initially unwelcomed by the authorities, though it was eventually accepted and suitable facilities provided. To begin with, householders were provided with a variety of options, some of which are still evident today. There was a simple reason for this, despite the cynical belief that it might be entirely attributable to parsimony and short-sightedness. The consequences of a single hit on a shelter housing dozens or hundreds of civilians were likely to be disastrous for morale, and it should not be supposed that the population enjoyed a universal resilience to the prospect of aerial bombardment.

By late 1940 the fact that people were beginning to leave the most heavily-assaulted cities was being reported in the popular press. Southampton had suffered particularly for a variety of reasons. It was a port, and the centre of the Supermarine industry. It was also on the south coast and extremely easy to find. The Bishop of Winchester is reported as having found on 2 December 1940 that 'everyone who can do so [is] leaving the town' (BZ2, 281). Margate, in East Kent, was very exposed to raids and even later in the war still suffered from hit-and-run sorties. The population of the town was about 40,000 in 1939 but this dropped by more than three-quarters as the war progressed. Of around 14,000 premises, more than 9,000 (64 percent) had been damaged. The choice made by many residents to move away is easy to understand.

In any case, evacuation of children fuelled a sense of foreboding from the outset, and the Government could not afford to risk large numbers of people fleeing from cities (at least conspicuously). There was also the question of time. Domestic shelters could be reached in seconds, and in circumstances where warnings of raids were unlikely to provide more than ten minutes notice this was a considerable advantage. The same considerations encouraged the use of semi-portable shelters made of concrete which were installed in factories, or even the remarkable iron cones devised as one-man fire-watcher shelters. The latter, secured to buried monolithic concrete blocks, looked like the nose cone of a rocket and must surely be one of the most extraordinary and now unfamiliar precautions against aerial bombardment. At any rate, it made sense to encourage people to stay where they were, protect their own property and look after themselves, albeit with official help and encouragement. The result was a variety of shelter facilities, with a varied manifestation in our own time.

The 'Refuge Room' was supposed to be a gas and splinter-proof room of an ordinary house, usually a cellar, made secure by minimizing windows and doors and reinforced with concrete. Brick walls would only do if reinforced with sandbags. The expectation of gas attack meant securing ventilation and thus the prospective refuge room builder was reminded that a room could only occupy fixed numbers of people for limited periods of time.

There were alternative precautions: the purpose-built shelter, normally erected far enough from housing to prevent damage from falling masonry, much the most dangerous of all the consequences of bombing. Option one was the trench. Recommended minimum depth was 1.4m, just deep enough to accommodate seated occupants. The idea was to roof it with wood or sheets of corrugated iron, and to secure the ends with blankets to create a 'gas curtain'.

Option two was to construct some sort of sunken or semi-sunken shelter, preferably with a superstructure of concrete and sheet-iron. Much the best known is of course the 'Anderson' shelter (named after Sir John Anderson, Minister of Home Security), many of which are still extant in back gardens across Britain.

The principle behind the Anderson shelter was to provide a cheap prefabricated structure which formed the shape and provided much of the strength. A trench was dug and into this the curved frames of corrugated iron sheet were erected. Exploiting the inherent strength of the arch, the curved roof transferred the downward force of the 0.6m-thick earth covering around the sides of the hut and into the ground. The basic design created a chamber 1.83m high, 2m long, and 1.37m wide. While it is obvious that something as basic as this could not withstand a direct hit, the Anderson proved to be an astonishingly durable precaution in spite of the susceptibility to damp (**83**). This is manifest in the numbers which survive, though these are steadily dwindling. However, with a little observation and care the debris of many others can be located, especially where gardens back onto woodland. Often, concrete fragments dumped over garden fences in this sort of place preserve the form of the corrugated sheets, themselves long since rotted away.

The discomfort caused by the Anderson and the sheer claustrophobic effect of hours cramped in the damp and cold led many people to stay at home and ignore the raids. To counter this, the Government also distributed the Morrison shelter which, far from being a structure, was no more than a modified piece of furniture. Appearing in 1941, the Morrison was a steel frame, big enough for several people to lie under but small enough to serve as a table of sorts. It was supposed to be strong enough to be able to support piles

83 An Anderson shelter shows its worth after a raid on 23 August 1940. Despite the evident damage it has survived better than the house its owners fled from

of fallen masonry. Naturally, these do not generally survive nowadays, having no practical value and being easily reclaimable as scrap.

Shelters like these were private, individual means of protecting homes and families. For larger groups of people, facilities like the caves in Chislehurst (Kent) were hardly likely to be widely available. The Government did provide a certain number of surface shelters, built of brick and concrete, in areas where there was no physical space for installing Anderson shelters or anything similar, or where there were no buildings with suitable basement facilities. The outcome illustrated the lack of real organization or even appreciation of what bombing could involve. Surface shelters were brick-built bunkers with flat concrete roofs and the appropriate specifications were issued in the spring of 1940, long before any bombing had taken place. The intention was to save resources and expedite construction and the result was to advise builders to favour lime in their mortar. Lime mortar is made of three parts sharp sand to one part lime. Cement mortar, which is much stronger, replaces the lime component with a mixture of chalk or limestone with clay or any other material containing silica and alumina. The outcome of the advice was that builders avoided using cement altogether and used lime mortar. This produced structures which looked the part but which had no capacity to absorb shock at all. Not only were the shelters constructed in the first wave hopelessly inadequate in this respect, but they also lacked any provision for lighting, water or sanitation. These all became very obvious shortcomings as night-long raids developed in the latter part of 1940. The only long-term solution was to build an additional skin of bricks with cement mortar around the shelters.

None of these precautions prevented bombing. They merely inhibited the ability of the Luftwaffe to cause as much damage as intended. In the final chapter of the book we will look at the nature of the evidence which can be gathered together to show the actual effects of bombing and what can be seen of that today.

7 The effects of bombing

Devastated city centres

The most obvious impact of sustained bombing of British cities was the destruction and damage to large areas of commercial and residential buildings. Throughout the 1950s and on into the 1970s some of the places laid waste were still very obvious, and in a few places they still are. But 60 years on from the beginning of the Blitz very little of this is evident in the same way. Just as an example, a major bomb-site on the south side of Ludgate Hill in the City of London served as a car-park right into the middle of the 1990s and allowed the north side to be bathed in sunlight for decades. It, too, has now disappeared beneath new office buildings. One of the ironies of the Blitz is that it opened up large zones of the City to the sun, creating an odd juxtaposition of light and air with ruin and destruction. Now once more the streets of the City have largely retreated to shadow.

Coventry's city centre, like that of many other devastated provincial towns, has of course been rebuilt but no effort was made to restore its original appearance in any sense. The old cathedral of St Michael's was famously left as a ruin (**78**), and joined to the new cathedral (eccentrically oriented just east of north-south) designed by Sir Basil Spence, erected in the 1950s. The outcome is a curious manifestation of past and present which would be extremely difficult to understand were one presented with the structures alone in an archaeological context. The physical structure of the old cathedral lacks its roof and almost all its internal features though the stumps of columns survive, as do incongruous fragments of stained glass in situ. Oddly, the tower escaped the conflagration of the 14/15 November 1940 and from certain angles it would be impossible to believe this had ever been the centrepiece of a catastrophic air-raid. The fire-damaged stone of the west wall of the south aisle contrasts with the adjacent unaffected stone of the tower, while a viewpoint from a few yards further west has scarcely altered in centuries (**84**). Yet, to approach the cathedral from the north-east is to do so through an epic complex of colossal concrete monstrosities which bear witness to the complete destruction of areas in this city.

Coventry has also suffered from economic swings in the last few decades. Despite this, renewal has often resulted in wholesale purging of city centre areas. Wine Street in Bristol was once a thoroughfare hemmed in by buildings on both sides. By the 1980s it had been transformed as a result of the effects of the night of 24/25 November 1940. One may regret the outright banality of some of the modern architecture, but it is undoubtedly more open and in some ways less claustrophobic than its pre-war appearance. Here, as in London and many other places, uncaptioned photographs of bombsites in the war are now often unidentifiable for the simple reason that rebuilding changed street orientation and obstructed views of landmarks in old pictures. The Barbican complex and the Paternoster

84 Coventry cathedral's south side from the west, looking along a scarcely-altered view

Square development (itself now earmarked for replacement) were only possible because of the large-scale clearances after the raids of 1940 and 1941. Physical evidence of bombing is now almost invisible.

Noble Street, in the north-west of the City, was almost entirely destroyed but ironically this had the effect of exposing the explanation for a hitherto-inexplicable kink in the medieval city walls. The medieval fortifications very largely reused the foundations and footings of the Roman city wall which enclosed an area of roughly 125ha. The kink in the Cripplegate area turned out to have been caused by the presence of a Roman fort, built possibly as early as around the year AD 90, which predated the Roman city walls built at least a century later. Probably housing the garrison of the Roman governor (though in fact there is absolutely no certainty about that at all), the fort was incorporated into the new walls by building up to the north-east corner, and then continuing from its south-west corner. As luck would have it, the south-west corner of the fort and the abutting city wall were exposed during the demolition of Victorian buildings in Noble Street wrecked in the Blitz. Consequently, the area was preserved as a small public park and gardens, now several metres below modern street level. The later brick walls sit on the Roman ragstone and mortar fortifications and even these, recognizable in photographs of the 1940s, have been left in situ providing an exceptional reminder of London's extraordinary past (**colour plate 24**).

London's City churches

Elsewhere, London's experiences of the Blitz are now less immediately obvious. St Augustine Watling Street, sited close to the south-east corner of St Paul's is, or was, one of the many churches built or rebuilt by Sir Christopher Wren in the fifty or so years following the Great Fire of 1666. That conflagration was followed by a similar, but less commercially driven, renewal and in the half-century after 1666 London emerged as a British version of a modern European city, though the elaborate plans by Wren, and also John Evelyn, were ignored in favour of a more piecemeal approach. St Augustine was in existence by 1148. By 1695 it had been completely rebuilt following the Fire, including a new spire, but over the succeeding centuries it was gradually engulfed by buildings (**85**). The Blitz made short work of almost all the buildings in the vicinity, including St Augustine's nave. Post-war clearance and development left the area very largely opened up, and the decision was made to leave what remained of the church as a feature of St Paul's churchyard, subsequently adapted to form part of a new structure for the cathedral choir school. Oddly though, even the present spire is a reproduction (**colour plate 27**).

St Augustine's is not the only City church preserved now just as a tower. Not far away, and in fact very close to Noble Street, is St Alban Wood Street. Occasionally Wren preserved or adapted a burnt church's pre-Fire appearance, even incorporating substantial parts of the medieval walls and concealing them by filling the windows and facing over the stone. In this case he produced a copy of the structure thought by some to have been designed by Inigo Jones, originally built between 1633–4. Even so, the church harked back to the Middle Ages in its Gothic style. The Blitz left a gutted ruin which strongly resembled the remains of the cathedral church St Michael's in Coventry. However, just as Coventry Cathedral was undergoing its transformation into a juxtaposition of death and rebirth, St Alban's was demolished apart from the tower which now stands, isolated, purposeless and incongruous, in the middle of the road, dwarfed by modern buildings (**86**).

Some churches were demolished and cleared away altogether though this was of course not exclusively caused by the Blitz. All Hallows Lombard Street was demolished by 1939 to make way for a new bank headquarters, though its tower was rebuilt as part of All Hallows, North Twickenham. St Swithin Cannon Street was a casualty of the war. Its ruins survived until 1962 when the site was cleared and now no trace exists at all. But the strangest fate of all must be that which befell St Mary Aldermanbury which once stood close to St Alban Wood Street at the junction of Aldermanbury and Love Lane. One of Wren's less prepossessing structures it, too, ended up as a gutted and roofless shell with an intact tower after the firestorm of 29/30 December 1940. The lower sections of the walls remain in situ, together with the stumps of columns, in a carefully laid-out garden. But the rest of what still stood in 1945 was systematically dismantled, sorted and numbered, and transported to Fulton in the state of Missouri. Here the church has been entirely rebuilt, restored and reopened as a place of worship and memorial to Winston Churchill. It thus enjoys the curious privilege of two physical manifestations (see BZ2, pp.554-9 for a comprehensive account of this work).

85 *St Augustine Watling Street around 1900. Built by Sir Christopher Wren between 1680–7. Not only have the surrounding buildings gone, destroyed in the Blitz, but so too has the main church building. Only the tower still stands* **(colour plate 27)**

86 St Alban Wood Street was destroyed in the Blitz. Now the tower stands isolated in the middle of the road

87 *Christ Church, Newgate, London. Built by Sir Christopher Wren between 1687–1704. Destroyed in the firestorm of 29/30 December 1940 this church exists now as a ruin, partially cleared for a road* (**colour plate 28**). *This view shows the church from the west in c. 1904*

Very few of the City churches or those in other parts of London have been left as they were when the war was over. St Anne, Soho, a church of uncertain pedigree (it may have been by Wren or William Talman), was yet another gutted ruin and tower. It now survives as a garden in what was once the nave while the 1803 tower built by Samuel Pepys Cockerell (descended from a relative of the diarist) still stands on the site. Christ Church Greyfriars Newgate is probably the most conspicuous ruin, standing as it does, very close to St Paul's and by a busy part of the City's one-way system. That it was not rebuilt was the occasion of some controversy because it was one of Wren's most extravagant creations (**87**). The extant ruins are certainly a powerful reminder of the destruction wrought in

1940–1 and easily the most conspicuous monument to the Blitz. But the church was rather less substantially destroyed than it looks. Much of the eastern section was summarily cleared away to make room for road widening, a policy we have all had time to appreciate and denigrate (**colour plate 28**).

Christ Church could have been rebuilt as many others were, such as St Bride's, Fleet Street (destroyed 29 December 1940), and St Clement Dane (destroyed 10 May 1941) amongst them. The latter still bears visible scarring from bomb damage on its outside walls (**88**), but otherwise its present state belies its wartime experiences. Nearby St Mary-le-Strand and, in the City, St Magnus the Martyr, escaped more or less unscathed. While these provide a basis for understanding the form and appearance of the churches which have been lost, it is the photographic archive which is the priceless record, illustrating above all else how impossible it is for the archaeologist to reconstruct the precise detail of ancient buildings known only from their foundations.

An unusual variation on the photographic record, and in some respects even more valuable, are the images in post-war feature films. The well-known Charles Crichton comedy *The Lavender Hill Mob* (1951) involves an elaborate robbery of gold bullion. Happily, much of the action is set in the City of London and a number of outdoor scenes record London's appearance in that year. About 30 minutes into the film an extensive sequence features the actor Stanley Holloway stationed as a lookout a few yards east of the ruins of St Nicholas Cole Abbey. Being gutted, lacking its steeple and window-less, the church is difficult to recognize except that the location and sculptural details confirm its identity. Panning shots in the same and other sequences show St Mary-le-Bow in Cheapside, Christ Church Newgate, and St Augustine Watling Street. The images provide a vivid and powerful record of the desolation in this part of the City, almost all attributable to the winter of 1940 and the first half of 1941. St Nicholas and St Mary-le-Bow have also been rebuilt and now, surrounded once more by buildings, they have been subsumed back into the sprawling mass of the City. Another of Crichton's films, *Hunted* (1952) stars a harassed murderer, played by Dirk Bogarde. Its first few minutes show the character skulking around the flats, warehouses, and wharves of a London that looks to a modern eye like a Third World disaster zone. Amongst the most conspicuous images are those of the ends of terraces where fireplaces and fractured walls of demolished sections have been consolidated with cement and concrete. To anyone growing up in London in the 1950s and 1960s these were very familiar sights.

Repairing the damage

Considering the requirements of new technology, it is easy to see why many buildings in the City of London would have been cleared away since the 1940s, regardless of whether they were destroyed by bombs. Nowadays it is not unusual for new commercial buildings to have a planned service life of only around a decade. Wren's churches were substantial masonry structures. Their fate lay in the wooden beams of their roofs and the extensive wooden fittings such as screens, pulpits, and seats. The same applied to the Guildhall. Once set alight the impact of incendiaries was all too plain, but it was normally the case

88 The north wall of St Clement Danes, Strand, in London showing deep Blitz scarring

that the basic wall structure of the churches survived, while the towers all seem to have been unusually resilient. Out in the suburbs, the consequences could be quite different. Brick-built, or older churches, like St Peter and St Paul in Bromley, wrecked on 16 April 1941, were more likely to suffer comprehensive structural failure.

Much of this kind of damage was due to the effects of blast, rather than the direct impact of a bomb. The outward pulse of air pressure left behind it a vacuum. Where a bomb fell in a road or any other open space close to housing, this caused the brick walls of the side facing the impact to explode outwards. For this reason, booklets and information sheets advised the reinforcement of windows with tape and sandbags and the bracing of internal walls. The potential damage was shown to devastating effect in flats and shops in Balham High Road on 14 October 1940 (**89**). Here a bomb struck the road and, despite the bomb continuing into the Underground railway tunnel below, the blast has pulled away outer walls right up to the top storey. With internal flooring thus deprived of partial support it is easy to see how the entire structure thus collapses or requires demolition. The classic effect of a bomb in a road was thus to destroy the façades of dozens of houses and to smash the glass of others.

A variety of solutions were applied to the problem, most of which provide distinctive evidence for the effects of the air war. Typically, houses were cleared where possible and the sites abandoned until peacetime. In extreme cases the opportunity was not lost on post-war planners who saw this as their chance to give over town centres to the motor car. In Park Lane, Croydon, a house erected in 1708 was reduced to its foundations after the

89 Classic Blitz damage in Balham High Road after Monday, 14 October 1940. The hole caused by the bomb has wrecked the road which has subsided into the Underground train tunnel beneath. Meanwhile blast damage has removed the façade from shops and flats overlooking the crater. Not surprisingly, the buildings were demolished. Where possible, new façades were built on to the framework

raid of 30 September 1940. Understandably it was not rebuilt, but the entire site has now been dug out to make way for a flyover.

Where damage was confined to the façades, houses were sometimes repaired in an approximate emulation of the style in the street concerned. Most of the houses affected were Victorian or Edwardian and these, especially those of after *c.* 1875 tended to have elaborate mouldings on front bays, usually in the form of floral-capped pilasters or columns, or some sort of decorative archway over the entrance. These features were unlikely to be replaced, at least in anything better than a pale imitation, producing a slightly shabby result where the new fronts look uncomfortable next to the originals.

In other cases the repair work is so authentic that there is effectively no clue to the incident. On 13 October 1940 a block of flats called Coronation Avenue at the north end of Stoke Newington Road was hit. At least one of the bombs struck the flats which was doubly unfortunate because many of the residents had crammed themselves into the basement bomb shelter. The bomb did not explode until it reached the ground floor, despite having passed through all the upper floors. The result, by the time the laborious job of clearing rubble had been completed, was the discovery that 154 people had been killed (mostly by drowning as mains water and sewage filled the shelter), many of whom are now commemorated on a special cenotaph at Abney Park Cemetery in Stoke Newington. The physical effect of the explosion was to create a complete gap in the block, right down to ground level. Subsequent rebuilding was only detectable from brick colour, creating an exact facsimile of the destroyed section.

Truncation, or adaptation, meant making something usable out of what remained without rebuilding or replacing. Holland House, a Jacobean mansion in Kensington dating to 1606, was burnt out in the early hours of 28 September 1940. All the upper floors, apart from the east wing, were destroyed. The latter remains in use and the rest of the house has been consolidated. Together with its gardens it remains open to the public, despite its appearance which makes it look like an elaborate garden folly.

Much more obvious than any of these examples are the intrusions of buildings of a wholly later style in a row of otherwise uniform houses. This is more likely to be attributable to the site being left vacant for many years after the war, and being used as car parks or scrapyards. Remarkably there are a few cases still evident today though these are more usually isolated buildings, evidently once part of a terrace that now stand in isolation. As recently as the 1980s the numbers were much greater. Generally speaking, the practice seems to have been to erect houses of more contemporary design, regardless of their overt incongruity. There are so many examples of this in London and other towns of England and Wales that they need no further description. The most extreme form of replacement is those cases where areas were entirely cleared and used for the erection of tower blocks.

There is one important caveat to interpreting sites of this date which exhibit damage, illustrating a classic archaeological problem. It is the case that where a general phenomenon can be observed, such as the burning of late Roman villas, one can speculate about a possible reason while never being able to specifically attribute any one instance to that cause. A bank near the Leytonstone High Road was photographed in a seriously damaged state in September 1940. Happily, its caption states that the damage was caused

90 The fear of aerial bombardment in the late 1930s led some householders to install their own concrete shelters well in advance of any government precautions. This example in Plaistow, Bromley (Kent), is so substantial that it has resisted post-war attempts to demolish it

by an exploding gas main. Otherwise, the attribution to Blitz damage would have been more or less automatic.

Relics of the Blitz

By the end of 1999 the Blitz had really started to recede from common recollection. By 2000 it subsists in the memory only of people who are well over 60 years old at the youngest, though for many people in their middle years childhood meant listening to endless stories from adults, for whom it had been an almost universal experience. In suburban gardens across the country, here and there, isolated air raid shelters still stand, often used as garden sheds or children's dens (**90**), their original purpose long forgotten. While the air war itself has found a new manifestation in the spruced and polished Spitfires that cavort at air shows and defy their venerable age, the Blitz belongs to the past as perhaps it should. In London the Imperial War Museum has a 'Blitz Experience' in which visitors are herded into a replica shelter and treated to darkness and noise before being led out into a replica ruined street. In fact remarkably convincing, it nevertheless provokes many visitors to spend much of their time stifling giggles. At London Bridge, a special museum is entirely given over to recreating life in London during the Blitz (**colour plate 29**). Surrounded by the wine bars and restaurants of converted wharfside warehouses it provides a scarce opportunity to enter a world of darkness, aircraft engine noise, explosions and confusion before emerging back into the turmoil of modern London.

As a collective human experience, the Second World War is unparalleled in history. It is as well to listen to the stories of those who were there while we can and combine them with the documentary and archaeological record. All of us, professionals and amateurs alike, have a great deal to learn from this epic period of modern history. For all its horror and inexpressible tragedy the invigorating and extraordinary challenges faced by everyone in that time have the power to still awe us all. This is perhaps becoming all the more pronounced as our tolerance and acceptance of risk of any sort diminishes almost by the day.

Epilogue

Elmer Bendiner served as a navigator with the US Eighth Air Force's 379th Bombardment Group at Kimbolton near Huntington. He took part in the Schweinfurt raids of August and October 1943 on Germany's ball-bearing plants. In these he witnessed the catastrophic losses suffered by the bomber crews and the horrifying susceptibility of a bomber to a determined and motivated fighter defence. Since the Second World War he has worked as a writer and journalist, recording his war experiences in The Fall of Fortresses *(1980), and lives in New York City.*

As a relic of the air war against the German onslaught of the 1940s, I am naturally engrossed not only in the living England, but in the past that lies just beneath the soil of the airbases that have returned to farmland, below the tar and gravel that refreshes the streets and highways, or nestles within the walls and foundations of pubs, cathedrals and row houses in a thousand hamlets and towns. Out of such unlikely stuff many people of my generation can conjure up an English battleground. That scene lives in the memories I share with many millions, tinged by the melancholy joy that leaps from the laughter of life on the edge of the unspeakable. It is a life that includes the utterly unacceptable death of comrades and those who in wartime appear and disappear before we know their names.

I imagine I can stir the entire past with the toe of my shoe in a field in Bedfordshire or in grass along a London embankment dimly lit by antique cars crawling with headlights cast down like overly modest maidens while beams of white light arc startlingly against the black sky.

In fact, however, I cannot scratch the past to light with the toe of my shoe, but must rely on the bulldozers and cranes and sifters of rubble that are the tools of archaeologists of war. For the air war was a conflict not only of men and women but a clash of machines, of things. We who remember them can scarcely call such machinery inanimate without an apology to them acknowledging the undeniable gallantry they exhibited.

My own plane, a graceful but somewhat battered B-17 Flying Fortress, called *Tondelayo*, lies at the bottom of the Channel. No matter. Every Spitfire, Lancaster, P-38 Lightning, B-24 Liberator, Focke-Wulf, Messerschmitt or any part of them, down even to stray spanners, or fragments of tails and twisted wings, are all part of that high drama that once played the stage of England.

Each metal fragment is as much a part of history as a Roman short sword found at the Wall, or a hair from the head of King Canute. Like each of us, it played a bit part in the drama. We are therefore intimately involved in the archaeologist's paydirt. Guy de la Bédoyère has not only described the exhumation of the props and sets of the drama of half a century ago, but he has also told the story of how Britain survived yet another cataclysm.

For many Americans he has documented the work of restoring a legend not to its pristine glories perhaps, but to glory nonetheless. Many of us knew a kind of England

91 Elmer Bendiner in 1943 with his B-17F, Tondelayo (42-29896), of the 379th Bombardment Group. The word 'Benny' above, marks the window through which he made his observations

before we saw it. We did not really suppose that the British inhabited a literary legend. Yet it was not merely our romantic imaginations that noted how well they fitted their fairy tales. The England I knew in my childhood was fashioned by, among others, Dickens, Thackeray, the Brontës, Saki, Gilbert and Sullivan, Shakespeare, Keats, Milton, Browning, Lewis Carroll, Captain Marryat, Edward Lear and St Nicholas Magazine. There were assorted knights in armour who tickled my boyish fancy, there were suffragists and rebels and villains like Richard III and Uriah Heep. My own country has enough legends and literature to delight any youngster but I had a voracious appetite in those days.

When I took leave of the skies to touch bases in England, Scotland, Wales and Northern Ireland it was only partly a literary exercise. There were fresh but familiar landscapes, bridges, pubs, towns, prisons, theatres and people who were sometimes charming and sometimes not so, frequently out of Hogarth or Rowlandson or Cruickshank or 'Spy' or Tenniel.

I have been back to Britain many times since the War, working or wandering. A trip never fails to recall the time when I was younger and at war and in England. Now they are stirring up the dust of those terrible and wonderful days. They are validating the past and Guy de la Bédoyère has shown us in loving and expert detail just how ghostly people and ghostly wings can be made to rise again. And for that this ghost is grateful.

Elmer Bendiner
New York, November 1999

Appendices

Appendix 1: museums and places to visit

Flying displays take place at many locations throughout the year, but almost all between Easter and October (**92**). They offer frequent, albeit expensive, opportunities to see Second World War aircraft flying though it must be said that many of the displays are similar and opportunities to view the machines close up is often very limited. Locations like Duxford that function as aviation museums as well usually levy substantially elevated admission prices on the day of an air show. Additional charges to enter enclosures nearer to the action have been controversial. The best place to find out what is on and where is in the various aviation enthusiasts' magazines, such as *Flypast*, which are readily available from high street newsagents.

Static displays of aircraft in museums obviously lack the dynamic of flight but they provide the chance for much more close-up examination. Note that opening hours and other details are bound to vary over time, though as up-to-date information as possible has been included here.

Cambridgeshire
Imperial War Museum,
Duxford Airfield,
Duxford CB2 4QR
Tel: 01223 835000

Derbyshire
Derby Industrial Museum,
Full Street,
Derby DE1 3AR
Tel: 01332 255308
Open: daily 10-5 (11 on Mondays, 2 on Sundays and Bank Holidays). Free (displays include several Rolls-Royce aero engines)

Norfolk
Thorpe Abbotts
100th Bombardment Group Association,
Common Road,
Dickleburgh, Diss
Norfolk IP21 4PH

92 Messerschmitt Bf 109G, known as 'Black 6', being prepared for an air display at Duxford. In the autumn of 1997 the aircraft was wrecked while performing another show at Duxford. The pilot was not seriously injured and the machine is now being restored for static display

Tel: 01379 740708
Open: all year at the weekend from 10 until 5 (4.30 in winter). Access to wartime control tower and numerous exhibits including engines, clothing, and armaments.

Isle of Wight
The Frontline and Aviation Museum, formerly at Sandown Airport, closed in late 1999. It is hoped that new premises will be found in Sandown in 2000.

Kent
Kent Battle of Britain Museum,
Aerodrome Road,
Hawkinge,
Folkestone, Kent CT18 7AG
Tel: 01303 893140
Open: daily Easter to the end of October 10-5, closing at 4 in October. Colossal quantities of wreckage from excavated aircraft and a number of full-size replicas. Photography and recording of any sort, including on paper, can lead to visitors being summarily ejected.

Manston Spitfire and Hurricane Memorial Building,
RAF Manston,
Ramsgate CT12 5BS
Tel: 01843 821940
Open: daily 10-5, closing at 4 from October to April. Selected displays of excavated

material, engines, ephemera, uniforms, and the immaculately restored Spitfire XVI, TB752.

Shoreham Aircraft Museum,
High Street,
Shoreham Village,
Sevenoaks, Kent TN14 7TB
Tel: 01959 524416
Open: 10-5 on Sundays only, May to September. Charming displays of excavated material in a small private museum often visited by pilots and other surviving aircrew. Access to the High Street by car is extremely limited and visitors should walk from as far as possible. Access by bus or coach is impossible.

London
Britain at War Experience
64-66 Tooley Street
London Bridge
Tel: 0207 403 3171
A short walk from London Bridge Underground and main line railway station
Open daily from 10am. Last admission 4.30 October to March, 5.30 April to September. Family tickets available. Displays and scenes of Blitz life in London.

Imperial War Museum,
Lambeth Road,
London SE1 6HZ (nearest Underground stations: Lambeth North and Waterloo)
Tel: 0207 416 5320
Open: daily, 10-6, except 24-26 December. Displays of original aircraft, including the wreckage of Hess's Messerschmitt Bf 110, and more detailed displays of life in Britain during the air war.

RAF Museum,
Grahame Park Way, Hendon,
London NW9 5LL (nearest Underground Station: Colindale)
Tel: 0208 205 2266
Open: daily 10-6 except Christmas and New Year. Vast numbers of aircraft (**93**) including the only intact extant examples of many Luftwaffe machines such as the Junkers Ju 88 and Heinkel He 111.

Science Museum,
Exhibition Road,
South Kensington
London SW7 2DD (nearest Underground station: South Kensington)
Tel: 0207 938 8080
Open: daily 10-6. Top-floor Flight Gallery features various British and German fighter

93 Spitfire V BL614, as displayed at RAF Hendon. This machine was recently restored at Rochester in Kent. It saw action in 1942 and 1943 with a variety of units, including participation in the disastrous raid on Dieppe on 19 August 1942

aircraft of the Second World War and cutaway engines. These include Hurricane I, L1592, which saw action in the Battle of Britain.

Sussex

Tangmere Military Aviation Museum,

Tangmere Airfield,

Chichester, W. Sussex PO20 6ES

Tel: 01243 775223

Open: daily 10-5.30 March to November, 10-4.30 February and November. Closed December and January. Displays of excavated material and a number of post-war aircraft as well.

Appendix 2: RAF Fighter Squadrons codes and aircraft serials

During the period in question operational RAF aircraft allotted to a squadron carried a three-letter code. The first two letters, paired on the pilot's side of the fuselage roundel, denoted the squadron. Thus **QV** represented No. 19 Squadron (**94**). The third letter identified the aircraft, and sometimes the pilot as well. Thus **QJ-S** was a Spitfire of No. 92 Squadron, normally flown by Allan Wright (**8**). As aircraft were replaced or moved about, so the third letter would be transferred to new machines. Thus Wright flew several Spitfires between 1940-1, each of which bore the letters **QJ-S**. The third letter was normally considered to be its call-sign. In Wright's case he considered the **S** to stand for Sheila or Satan, but Sugar, O-Orange, or T-Tommy were more normal. In some instances senior officers were permitted to use letters corresponding to their initials. Robert

94 *Spitfire I, X4474, of No. 19 Squadron, as indicated by the* **QV** *fuselage code. The aircraft was with No. 19 at Duxford from 20 September 1940 until 5 October, thus fixing the period in which the picture was taken. It survived the war and was allocated to the Royal Danish Air Force. This was cancelled and its later history unrecorded. It was probably scrapped*

Stanford Tuck's Spitfire V in which he was shot down in January 1942 while wing leader at Biggin Hill carried the mark **RS-T**. In one variation from this pattern a question mark, **?**, was used by the commanding officer of some squadrons beginning with No. 245 Squadron (Freeman 1998, 32).

The squadron letters were subject to change. No. 92 Squadron carried the codes **GR** during the Battle of France. These were changed to **QJ** shortly afterwards, perhaps (as Wright suggests) to avoid creating the impression that the squadron was charged with protecting the monarch ('Georgius Rex'). However, **QJ** was also the code used by No. 616 Squadron at the time, but this duplication seems to have been disregarded.

Squadrons were divided amongst the four Groups of Fighter Command. Each had their individual bases. Thus for example, No. 19 Squadron was based at Duxford and fell within No. 12 Group. However, squadrons were moved about as required and even on a given day they might operate from a forward base, such as Hawkinge, having been sent there from their normal base. Aircraft were liable to be involved in action almost anywhere in the south-east once airborne. It is possible to compile lists of which squadrons were based where but the product is only valid for a single day.

Every aircraft carried its own serial number, allocated from a block. No other machine ever carried this number. Thus *R6753* was a Spitfire I belonging to No. 603 Squadron, and which carried the letters **XT-G**. Its demise on 29 August 1940 meant that **XT-G** was transferred to another machine but *R6753* was not used again. Useful summary lists of squadron markings, and the division between the Groups that formed Fighter Command, can be found in Franks (1997, 160-3).

Fighter serials (Spitfires and Hurricanes only)
It is fairly obvious that serial numbers were allocated almost randomly from 'available' blocks. Thus the Spitfire Mark I P-series had higher numbers than the later Spitfire Mark II P-series. Not all these listed below were either manufactured before or during the Battle of Britain or even ever saw service in action. Individual aircraft were also withdrawn for testing, and conversion to the specification of higher marks.

The Spitfire I model was issued with serial numbers drawn from the following blocks:
K9787-9999
L1000-1096
N3023-3299
P9305-9567
R6595-7257
X4009-4997
AR212-261

The Spitfire II model was issued with serial numbers drawn from the following block:
P7280-8729

The Hurricane I was issued with serial numbers drawn from the following blocks:
L1547-2146
N2318-2729
P3265-3984
R2680-2689
V6533-7195, 7200-8127
W6667-6670
Z6983-7162 (Canadian-built)

Appendix 3: the Luftwaffe and its identification marks

The specifications, particularly of the Luftwaffe aircraft, varied somewhat during the period in question. Moreover, the various reference sources available all vary in minor detail as well. Despite laborious attempts to collate some sort of meaningful summary of specifications the effort proved futile, due to the extraordinary rate of discrepancies between different reference works. In any case, figures for speed, range and ceiling are largely theoretical. Use of emergency boost, combat conditions, and heavy winds could all severely reduce range by using up fuel at much higher rates. For more information some of the better sources for these and a much wider range of aircraft include Mondey (1994 and 1996) and Townshend Bickers (1990).

If the RAF squadron code system seems arcane, the Luftwaffe system of aircraft markings was equally incoherent. I am grateful to Simon Parry for providing guidance.

Markings consisted of a pair of characters on either side of the black Luftwaffe cross. The first two characters denote the squadron (Geschwader). The fourth letter marked the

95 Messerschmitt Bf 110 of ZG26, as indicated by the fuselage code **U3**. *The exact aircraft is not identifiable but the unit took part in the Battle of Britain*

flight (Staffel) to which the aircraft belonged within that squadron (though squadron and flight are far from exact equivalents). The flights themselves were organized into groups (Gruppen) within the squadron but these were fixed and did not need marking. The third letter identified the aircraft within the flight.

There were several different classifications of squadrons in the Luftwaffe, the main ones of which were (translations should not be interpreted as meaning the same as the English terms; a Luftwaffe squadron did not resemble an RAF squadron, for example):
ErpGr = Erpobungs Gruppe — experimental test wing
JG = Jagdgeschwader — fighter squadron
LG = Lehr Geschwader — instruction/development squadron
KG = Kampfgeschwader — bomber squadron
KGr = Kampfgruppe — bomber wing
StG = Stuka Geschwader — divebomber squadron
ZG = Zerstoerergeschwader — destroyer fighter squadron

Thus a Dornier Do 17 carrying the markings **F1+DT** which crashed at Leaves Green, near Biggin Hill, on 18 August 1940 means that it was aircraft **D**, belonging to No. 9 Staffel (**T** = 9) where **F1** happens to be the code of KG (Kampferbände Geschwader = Bomber Squadron) no. 76 (**25**). The Geschwader sequence was random, thus **5J** denoted KG4, and **B3** KG54. Messerschmitt Bf 110s of ZG no. 26 bore the markings **3U** (**95**).

The flights were organized into groups (Gruppen) within the Squadron but as these were fixed, this did not need indicating. **H**, **K**, and **L** were flights 1, 2 and 3 of Gruppe I,

M, **N**, and **P** were flights 4, 5, and 6 of Gruppe II, and **R**, **S**, and **T** were flights 7, 8, and 9 of Gruppe III. Thus the Dornier from Leaves Green belonged to No. 9 Staffel of Gruppe III within KG76. Fourth letters **A** to **G** were allocated to aircraft belonging to staff (Stab) flights of any given squadron. The production (Werk) number, if visible, was painted on to the tailplane.

Ramsey (1988, 17) has more detailed information.

Appendix 4: ranks

Luftwaffe — RAF (approximate equivalents)
Oberst = Group Captain
Oberstleutnant = Wing Commander
Major = Squadron Leader
Hauptmann = Flight Lieutenant
Oberleutnant = Flying Officer
Leutnant = Pilot Officer

Feldwebel = sergeant
Gefreiter = aircraftsman, first class

(n.b. Ober at the beginning of a German rank indicates a higher status of that rank)

Appendix 5: excavating aircraft

By law military aircraft of British origin which crash in the UK are Crown property. It does not matter where they crash, or on who owns the land. However, the Ministry of Defence may elect to dispose of the aircraft's remains, if they are still on or in the ground, by awarding a licence to dig. The same applies to German aircraft, treated as the spoils of war. United States aircraft are US property, but dealing with their remains is administered by the Ministry of Defence. Where an aircraft is believed to contain human remains, it is not apparently normal for permission to be granted. It is also the case that where potentially lethal ammunition or bombs might be involved, various restrictions and legal requirements cover their safe excavation and disposal.

Abbreviations and select bibliography

Abbreviations

BofB V: Ramsey 1989 (see below)
BZ1, BZ2, and BZ3: Ramsey 1987, 1989 (ii), and 1990
MS: Morgan and Shacklady 1987
V12: a twelve-cylinder engine divided into two parallel banks of six sharing a common crankshaft. From the front or back the arrangement is V in shape with the crankshaft at the bottom and each bank of cylinders forming either side of the V. This was the form of the Roll-Royce Merlin engine. The German Jumo and Daimler-Benz engines were inverted V12s which means the design was simply upside down, thus ?.

Select bibliography

There are so many books available on aspects of Second World War aviation that it is impossible to do more than list a very few here. These, however, have proved the most useful in the preparation of this book and include a number published during the war years.

Anon., *The Battle of Britain. An Air Ministry Account of the Great Days from 8th August–31st October 1940* (HMSO) London 1941

Anon., *Front Line 1940-41. The Official Story of the Civil Defence of Britain* (HMSO) London 1942

Baxter, G.G., Owen, K.A. and Baldock, P., *Aircraft Casualties in Kent. Part 1: 1939 to 1940* (Meresborough Books) Rainham 1990

Bowyer, M.J.F., *Aircraft for the Few* (Patrick Stephens) Sparkford 1991

Bowyer, M.J.F., *Aircraft for the Many* (Patrick Stephens) Sparkford 1995

Brooks, R.J., *Kent Airfields in the Second World War*, Countryside Books, Newbury 1998

Brown, R., *Shark Squadron. The History of 112 Squadron 1917–1975* (Crécy Books) [no town stated] 1994

Catling, Skene, *Vanguard to Victory. An account of the first months of the British Expeditionary Force in France* (Methuen) London 1940

Cato, *Guilty Men* (Gollancz) London 1940

Charlwood, D., *No Moon Tonight* (Goodall Publications) Wilmslow 1984 (reprinted 1995, originally published in 1956)

Clostermann, P., *The Big Show* (Chatto and Windus) London 1951

Dawson, A., 'An Introduction to the "Tealby" Issue of Henry II', in *Coins and Antiquities*, August 1999

Deighton, L., *The Battle of Britain* (Jonathan Cape) London 1980

Ellis, K., *Wrecks and Relics* (Midland Publishing) Leicester

Elstob, P., 'One Man's Blitz' in *The Illustrated History of World War II*, Volume 2, ed. B. Liddell Hart (BPC Publishing) London, 244 1973

Evan-Hart, J., 'From Jurassic Fangs to Wild Mustangs' in *Treasure Hunting*, November 1999

Fellowes, P.F.M., *Britain's Wonderful Air Force* (Odhams Press) London *c.*1942

Franks, N.L.R., *Royal Air Force Fighter Command Losses of the Second World War, Volume 1 Operational Losses: Aircraft and Crews 1939–1941* (Midland Publishing) Leicester 1997

Freeman, R.A., *The Fight for the Skies* (Arms and Armour) London 1998

Gibson, G., *Enemy Coast Ahead* (Michael Joseph) London 1946 (and numerous reprints)

Grey, C.G., *Bombers* (Faber) London 1941

Harvey-Bailey, A., *The Merlin in Perspective — the combat years* (Rolls-Royce Heritage Trust) Derby 1995 (4th edition)

Hillary, R., *The Last Enemy* (Macmillan and Co.) London 1942 (frequently reprinted)

Hough R., and Richards, D., *The Battle of Britain* (Hodder and Stoughton) London 1989

Irwin, A., *Infantry Officer* (Batsford) London 1943

Jackson, R., *Spitfire. The Combat History* (Airlife) Shrewsbury 1995

Kaplan, P., and Collier, R., *The Few. Summer, 1940. The Battle of Britain*, (Greenwich Editions) London 1996

Kingcome, B., *A Willingness to Die* (Tempus) Stroud 1999

Lord, W., *The Miracle of Dunkirk* (Allen Lane) London 1982

Martin, H., *Battle* (Gollancz) London 1940

McLachlan, I., *Final Flights* (Patrick Stephens Limited) Sparkford 1989

Meacock, F.T., 'Airframe construction' in *Air Training Manual* (Odhams) London *c.*1941

Mondey, D., *British Aircraft of World War II* (Chancellor Press) London 1994

Mondey, D., *Axis Aircraft of World War II* (Chancellor Press) London 1996

Morgan, E.B., and Shacklady, E., *Spitfire. The History* (Key Publishing) Stamford 1996

Perry, C., *Boy in the Blitz* (Colin A. Perry) Cirencester 1980

Price, A., *Spitfire. A Documentary History* (Macdonald and Jane's) London 1977

Price, A., *The Hardest Day* (Mcdonald and Jane's) London 1979

Price, A., *Spitfire at War 3*, London 1990

Price, A., *The Spitfire Story* (Arms and Armour) London 1995 (2nd edition)

Quill, J., *Spitfire* (John Murray) London 1993 (reprinted by Arrow Books, 1985)

Ramsey, W.G. (Ed), *The Blitz Then and Now, Volume 1 September 3, 1939–September 6, 1940*, After the Battle Magazine, London 1987

Ramsey, W.G. (Ed), *The Blitz Then and Now, Volume 2 September 7, 1940–May 1941*, After the Battle Magazine, London 1989(i)

Ramsey, W.G. (Ed), 1989, *The Battle of Britain Then and Now*, After the Battle Magazine, London 1989(ii) (5th edition)

Ramsey, W.G., (Ed), *The Blitz Then and Now, Volume 3 May 1941–May 1945*, After the Battle Magazine, London 1990

Richey, P., *Fighter Pilot. A personal record of the Campaign in France September 8th, 1939, to June 13th, 1940* (Batsford) London (published anonymously in 1941, and in his name in subsequent editions)

Saunders, A., 'Wreck Recovery in 1940' in *After the Battle*, no. 34

Saunders, A., 'Is the RAF Museum Hurricane a genuine Battle survivor?' in *Flypast*, February 2000 issue, 99

Scutts, J., *Spitfire in action*, Squadron/Signal publications Aircraft no. 39, Carrollton, Texas 1980

Shepherd, C., *German Aircraft of World War II* (Sidgwick & Jackson) London 1979

Shirer, William L., *Berlin Diary*, (Hamish Hamilton) London 1941

Shores, C., and Williams, C., *Aces High* (Grub Street) London 1994

Shores, C., *Aces High, Volume 2*, (Grub Street) London

Smith, D.J., *High Ground Wrecks and Relics* (Midland Publishing) Leicester 1997 (4th edition)

Stevens, S.G.L. (forthcoming), 'Archaeological Investigations at Hawkinge Aerodrome, Hawkinge, Kent'

Terraine, J., *The Right of Line. The Royal Air Force in the European War 1939–1945* (Hodder and Stoughton) London 1985

Thole, Lou., 'Underground Luftwaffe' in *Flypast*, February 1999, 103-7

Townshend Bickers, R., *The Battle of Britain* (Ted Smart) Godalming 1990

Waln, N., *Reaching for the Stars* (The Cresset Press) London 1939

Woodley, M., 'Travels in Vietnam', in *Flypast*, April 1999, 25-27

Index

(ranks given are normally those held during the Battle of Britain)